PARADOX
Developing Your Influence Through Surrender

Jason M. Bachman

Talking Donkey Press

WILLARD, MISSOURI

Copyright © 2015 by **Jason M. Bachman**

All rights reserved. No part of this publication may be reproduced, distributed or transmitted in any form or by any means, without prior written permission.

Talking Donkey Press
Willard, Missouri
www.jasonmbachman.com

Publisher's Note:
Additional Resources can be found at jasonmbachman.com

Cover by Jonathan May - http://jonathanisaac.com/

Edited by Bethany Dixon

Bible verses used from www.blueletterbible.com

Book Layout © 2014 BookDesignTemplates.com

Paradox – Developing Your Influence Through Surrender/ Jason M. Bachman. -- 1st ed.
ISBN 978-0-9968535-0-7

Dedicated to my wife, Natalie.

I have come to set the world on fire, and I wish it were already burning!

—JESUS

CONTENTS

THE FIRST OPTION 1
   "It's Easier Said than Done" 2
   Was it A Waste? 2
   That Might Work for Others 3
   What Happens Next? 4
   Why is This Important? 5
THE HOPE COAT 7
   Hope is All Around Us 8
   The Foundation of Hope 9
   Attitude is Everything 11
GOD'S BEEN THERE BEFORE 13
   What is Faith? 14
   This Seems Impossible 14
   What's Next? 15
   Why is it Worth It? 17
LISTEN UP 19
   Calibrating the Heart 20
   Measure Twice, Cut Once 21
   Free Words 22
   Marketing the Heart of God 23
MICROMANAGING THE HOLY SPIRIT 25
   I Want to Believe 27
   What Now? 29
THE REBEL AND THE HEIR 31

 The Identifier 32
 Living on Empty 33
 Weaken Your Personal Rebellion.....................................34
 Don't Be Fooled..36
DEFEATING THE DICTATOR 37
 The Path of Least Resistance 38
 Indicators that Your Will is Alive.......................................39
 There Is Hope..40
JAILBREAK...43
 Releasing Me 44
 Being Close to the Enemy 44
 Wise as a Snake 47
RELENTLESS PURSUIT 49
 What Does Freedom Look Like?.......................................50
 What's the Alternative? 51
 What Will I Need to Do for Freedom? 52
 Living in a New Reality...52
 The Blessing of Freedom 53
INDESTRUCTIBLE 55
 A Broken Body, an Indestructible Spirit 56
 Coping with Loss 56
 Pain: the Great Distractor 57
 Constant Healing...58
SAME OLD RUT? 63
 Living Out of the Ruts 64
 Good Things Happen 65
 Learning Transformation 66
 Don't Get Stuck 67

THE RIGHT PERSPECTIVE	69
Changing the Meaning	70
Failure is not Final	72
The Benefit of Surrendered Perspective	73
CONTAGIOUS PEACE	75
The Silent Killer	76
The Solution	77
Let It Go	78
Contagious Peace	78
LINCOLN LOGS OR LUMBER?	81
Aftermath of Devastation	82
The Building Materials	82
Built to Last	83
A Last Word on Dealing With Pressure	85
IN MEMORY OF	87
The Legacy of the Holy Spirit	88
Imitate What Is Important	90
He leads. We follow.	91
He Empowers. We Experience.	92
ARE YOU GOOD ENOUGH?	93
God's Way	94
The Biggest Obstacle of All	95
Listen Closely and Follow Correctly	96
God Provides	97
THE UNBELIEVER'S IDENTITY	99
Identity Revealed	100
The Obstacle of Me	101
LUNATICS FOR SURVIVAL	103

- Healed the First Time 105
- Rich's Story 106
- When You've Done Everything, Just Stand 107
- I'LL DO IT BETTER 111
  - Nothing Changed 111
  - Don't Do That Again 112
  - The Mirror Image 113
  - Learn to Discern 115
- I'M IN MY OWN WAY 117
  - New Levels 118
  - Growing in the Middle of Success 119
  - Credit Makes Enemies. Let's Stay Friends 120
  - Don't Be Afraid of the Dirt 121
- SPINACH OR KRYPTONITE? 123
  - Finding Strength 124
  - Just Show Up 124
  - Not Alone 125
  - How to Walk 126
  - Playing it Safe Never Changed the World 128
- THIS ISN'T WHAT I HAD IN MIND 129
  - The Biggest Letdown of All 130
  - Resurrection Intent 131
  - The Butterfly Effect 131
  - The Obstacle to Resurrection 133
- SO THAT'S WHAT IT LOOKS LIKE! 135
  - The Magician's Volunteer 136
  - God's Not a Magician 136
  - The Greatest of These is Love 137

This is What it Looks Like 139
FEARLESS AGRESSION 141
   Getting Back on the Horse 142
   Redirect the Fear 143
   How Would I Think Differently? 143
   Perfected Love 145
GO THROUGH THE FIRE 147
   Fiery Zeal 148
   The Other Aspect of Fire 148
   Fire Extinguishers 149
   How We Know What is Important 150
   The Fire of Desire 151
THE GLASS IS ALWAYS HALF-FULL 153
   The Best Possibilities are the Ones that Require Endurance
   157
WHAT REALLY MATTERS 159
   Extreme Effort 160
   Ignoring the Bright and Shiny 161
   What Really Matters 162
   Practicing the End in Mind Mentality 163
TREASURE IN CLAY JARS 165
   The Art of Community 166
   Treasure Hunters 166
   The IMAGE of God 167
   See God's Perspective 169
iCARE 171
   If Compassion is so Great, Why is it so Difficult? 171
   Who Qualifies for My Care? 172
   How the Holy Spirit Changes Me 173

One Thing to Keep in Mind 174
You'll See a Difference 174
HERE WE GO 177
Measuring Tools 178
Your Next Steps 180

INTRODUCTION

What's worse—watching potential remain inactive while purpose waits to be filled or seeing construction workers outnumber the needs of a job? In both scenarios, people are disengaged from bringing a solution to a situation. But we don't always see missing potential like we see an overabundance of workers. I am convinced that everything this world needs to become more like God's kingdom lies dormant in places where purpose needs to be fulfilled. The perception that the job is already being done blocks the fulfillment of purpose. Something is missing. The world-changers have become disengaged from perspective and mission while being distracted by seemingly good activities.

This book may change that. Key to any movement is a strong leader. There is always one person with an idea who can communicate it from thought to action. The key leader in a movement of transformation is the Holy Spirit. He is the ultimate leader, coach, director, and friend. My aim is to present a picture of what a movement led by the Holy Spirit could look like and make it plain so you can run with it.

I've discovered that God likes to work through people who couldn't possibly receive credit for accomplishing the things they did. The Bible is full of examples:

- God chose Paul, the most religious of all Jewish rabbis, to bring the message of salvation to the Gentiles.
- The Spirit performed miracles through Peter who had a serious issue with self-control.
- God chose David, a young boy to lead a nation based on the contents of his heart, not the qualities of his appearance.
- God chose Moses, a man who stuttered and had previously fled the country, to return to that country to

release captives from bondage and lead them into freedom.

Today God uses people who are connected to his Spirit to live strong lives, be inspirations to others, and humbly acknowledge God's greater work within them. They are people who have fought for *dependence* and won. Surrender isn't passive. Resisted surrender means saying, "Well, I guess I've tried everything; now I'll let God try something." Aggressive surrender is an intentional effort to depend completely and totally upon God for all that is needed to live and to be earthen vessels that the Holy Spirit flows through. Jesus gave an example of dependence upon God when he did nothing except what he saw the Father do: first *surrender*; second, *minister*.

It is much easier for a river to flow in a bed clear of obstacles than around rocks, fallen trees, sand bars, and bends. If your life is a river bed and the Holy Spirit is the river, what does your river bed look like—clear or cluttered?

God is looking for touchpoints on this earth to bring freedom, hope, healing. God touches the earth through people who willingly work with Him to accomplish eternal purposes. God chooses to work through you and me. Given our pasts and propensity for screwing things up, it's amazing we hold credibility in God's eyes. God's work through us is not based on us; it's based on the Holy Spirit and His ability to equip, empower, restore, and transform. Therefore, we need to redirect our efforts from trying to impress a holy God with our abilities and sacrifices to aggressively surrendering to the plan, purposes, and direction of God through the Holy Spirit. The effort lies not in the production of the hands and feet but in the alignment of the will to the heart of God.

Good people can do great things yet not be completely surrendered to their greatest potential. Even Jesus' disciples experienced greatness while ministering with Him during His time on earth, yet their greatest potential remained to be discovered until Christ ascended to heaven and the Holy Spirit took His place. Their surrendered pursuit of the Holy Spirit gave them the ability to begin a movement 2,000 years ago. What Jesus did *for* them and *with* them, the Holy Spirit did *through* them. They became the first touchpoints on earth for God to work His plan of ultimate redemption. Their true aggressive surrender was the model for a partnership defined by intentional listening, willing action, and faith based upon a limitless God.

Notes: 1) Learning and discovery without progress only puff up the intellect and leave the inner person unchanged. Application is the key. Reading books about fitness and body stewardship does little unless accompanied by sweat, soreness, and the subtle irritation of having to get up earlier than normal. 2) You notice progress when the shiny things fail to impress you as much as the eternal things leave you in awe. 3) This surrender thing may be the hardest thing you'll ever do. Don't be surprised by the challenges you will face from the enemy. 5) This surrender thing may be the best thing you'll ever do and may create within you more peace, joy, and love than you could have imagined. 6) Finally, you may be part of turning a world upside down... or right-side up, depending on your perspective.

Take courage in this potential unknown season. You may be launched into places you have no business being on your own. You may experience wholeness to an extent you never thought possible. You may help facilitate restoration in situations that seemed irreparably broken. The level of your aggressive surrender is proportionate to the possibility of God's work in you and through you. Will you join the fight for dependence?

CHAPTER ONE

THE FIRST OPTION

My fights could be measured in seconds. They were more like standoffs with a few punches thrown in for good measure. One fight ended with the other guy's bloody nose. Another fight ended with me unable to breathe. I've been sucker kicked before. It happened on a Sunday school bus ride to church. I don't remember the words that caused the boot to my face. The kid who kicked me had some serious flexibility. Maybe he was a ninja.

I've won many wrestling matches because I hate losing. That's what pushed me to lose weight, work hard in practice, and focus on my opponent. Out of all the competitive events that I've been in, the one thing that infuriated me the most was losing a Bible quiz match. Of all things to be a good sport in, this would be it, right? I guess I didn't know how to lose graciously.

We have the choice to unconditionally surrender to the Holy Spirit. Surrender is usually associated with defeat and avoided at all costs. Spiritual surrender isn't built from that foundation. Spiritual surrender is built on trust. Active surrender precedes deep influence. Deep influence is forged in the furnace of developed trust. When we give God the ability to work in us through our trust, He empowers us to make a great difference. Surrender built from trust in the Holy Spirit helps us learn how to overcome all things.

"It's Easier Said than Done"

People who say, "It's easier said than done" don't believe that God can be trusted with their complete and total devotion. It can be difficult to trust God with our sacrifice. It can also be difficult to trust God with our pain. How will we know for sure that our sacrifice means something? How will we know for sure that our pain was worth something?

At some point in our lives, we face the decision to surrender unconditionally. We have the choice to completely surrender to the work of God in us or refuse the influence of His Holy Spirit. Because of God's character, we can be certain that our surrender will bring freedom and unlimited power through the work of His Spirit. Surrender in a human conflict means an end to the fight. Spiritual surrender, on the other hand, provides strength for the fight of faith.

The action of unconditional surrender never begins with a deed. It begins with a decision. At what point will you determine to trust God and give Him access to the decisions of your life?

Was it A Waste?

In 1955, five young missionaries moved their families to South America to reach a tribe of people. They were known for being fearsome warriors and had very little contact with the outside world. The missionaries trusted God and responded to His call instead of staying home and playing it safe. Once in South America, the men began to initiate contact with the tribe. Communication was difficult because of the language barrier. In time, they began communicating and planned a meeting. The meeting place was remote, so they flew in a hydroplane for a river landing.

Something went wrong during that meeting. The tribe killed the five young men and destroyed their plane. Searchers discovered the bodies and relayed the information back to the families. The national media sensationalized their deaths. Some reporters declared their deaths as a waste of lives. These men were following the call of God and trusting Him with their lives. Why would God allow such a thing to happen? Jim Elliot, one of the men who was killed, wrote a phrase that has inspired me for years: *He is no fool who gives what he cannot keep to gain what he cannot lose.*

What some considered a waste, God considered a seed. Years after this incident, my dad traveled to Ecuador on assignment. He met a man who was a young boy when the bodies of these missionaries were brought into the city, spears still stuck in their bodies. That young boy is now a pastor. God's seed of five young missionaries planted a movement of people who serve God and trust Him. Those young missionaries had a surrendered mindset: they knew that trusting God was easier *done* than *said*. Their actions spoke volumes over any words they could say.

That Might Work for Others

Jesus told His disciples that they should expect pain and trouble on this earth, but He also told them not to worry because He had overcome this world. Jesus was preparing them to deal with their broken expectations of His soon coming death. How does this work for me? Trusting God is hard if you're working from a foundation of trauma. Pain is poor building material to build a foundation for trust. Building trust begins by accepting healing from traumatic situations. Accepting God's ability to redeem is crucial.

There might be a situation in your life that you've never really gotten over. That situation is holding you back from completely trusting God. Perhaps there's a deep thread of resentment that blames Him for allowing it to happen. What if you were able to think about it in a different way? God is a good redeemer. He takes what appears lifeless and gives it new life. He can take what appears hopeless and infuse hope. Even if the situation cannot be changed, at least the hurt can be healed. Consider what might be holding you back. It may have just crossed your mind. Trust in God's ability to redeem and you can build a foundation for a complete surrender to freedom.

What Happens Next?

I used to be on staff at a church. One Sunday morning, I prayed for the offering and gave a short example of how God works in our lives when we trust Him with our money. The following week, I was approached by a man who told me, "I raised my hand on Sunday in agreement with what you said about God protecting us from the devourer. It was the first time that I decided to take a risk like that. This week my car broke down and now we have to put money into it. Why would that happen if I decided to trust God?" I was at a loss for what to say.

I wish I could have told him what I've learned now. Decisions to trust God are always tested. How good is a chair that you cannot sit on? How effective is trust that cannot come through the fire? Untested trust is no trust at all. God can be trusted to take us through the fire. Being tested isn't necessarily a bad thing. Occasionally, it takes a fire to burn off restraints and reveal great value. What may be restraining you now needs to be incinerated in a fire of testing to release the treasure God has placed in you.

Why is This Important?

Trusting God with complete and unconditional surrender will make way for the supernatural to become normal. God answering your prayers goes from being a big deal to something that is expected. This new expectation is not entitlement; it gives God room to do what He needs to how He needs to do it. When we trust God with our whole heart, we learn about His character and His abilities. An increased perspective of God makes everything else seem very small. Trials and things prayed and hoped for actually pale in comparison the glory of God that can be revealed through our trust in Him.
Trusting God creates a paradigm shift and a perspective change. That is worth the effort for first-option trust. Trusting God *first* is better than trusting Him *last* after you've tried everything else. If you choose to surrender, God will take you places you've never imagined and help you to be the person He's always known you could be.

CHAPTER TWO

THE HOPE COAT

We almost didn't complete our hike near Fountain Hills, AZ. Our group had the best of intentions and planned accordingly, but temperatures in the low 100s can change a simple hiking trip into a dangerous situation. The beginning of the journey was easy. We crossed the river in rafts and climbed up the trails with ease. As the day warmed up, our water supply decreased, but when we decided to turn around and head back, it still appeared that we were in good shape.

When it is over 100 degrees with an Arizona sun, a person can become dehydrated without even noticing. When the body stops sweating and the skin turns clammy, you're in trouble. Heat-related injuries soon follow. Being overheated is like being on fire with no way to extinguish it. When dealing with desert heat, you always have to be prepared for the worst. Thankfully, we made our way back to the vehicles with no injuries. Had we been out in the desert for another half hour, however, this story wouldn't have ended so happily.

Summer and winter environments can be dangerous. Being unprepared for those environments is an invitation for disaster. Being prepared for the brutal environments of life comes with wearing the proper attire. The same is true with our spiritual lives. The right attire to deal with the "stuff" of life is hope. Hope is a chosen attitude and a mentality that helps a person get through difficult circumstances. Hope is the difference between overcoming tough environments and becoming victims of circumstance.

Hope is All Around Us

Convoy of Hope is a faith-based organization that provides hope. At the time of this writing, I've personally directed nearly thirty compassion events reaching out to some of the most destitute people across the United States. Poverty can erode hope, but even a force as strong as poverty cannot compare with hope supplied by another person through God's love.

Hope is not the solution to change situations. Hope is the insulation that protects us from the conditions of those situations. Hope must be activated to be effective. The person who is surrendered to the direction of the Holy Spirit realizes their hope is built on the ability of God, not in the uncertainty of the outcome.

Rose was the type of person that had been written off. People gave her no hope to change or become the person God intended for her to be. She was one who came to a Convoy of Hope event for the first time and experienced a love she'd never known before. Volunteers at the event demonstrated love that opened her heart to the work of God. It took Rose a couple of years to surrender her will and heart to God. Once she aligned her life with God's, she began to wear the hope coat. Through hope, she expected a better life that God could provide. She now demonstrates hope through her life to other broken people who've lost hope along the way.

Rose is an example of placing hope in the right place. Her situation was beyond human repair and needed deep intervention. The Holy Spirit's work in her life was activated through hope. She began to hope for something better and gave God something to work with. She chose to hope in God.

The Foundation of Hope

Up north, people grow weary of the snow when winter stretches into April. During the long winters, snow arrives in October and remains well into March. March is the month that brings hope to the northerners as days grow longer and the temperatures rise. March can also bring great disappointment with another blizzard. People get grumpy when their hope has been placed in spring only to be met with another dose of winter. Smiles disappear when snow covers the sidewalks.

There are some seasons in life that seem to never end. During those times, it is tempting to place hope in the wrong source. Just when you think things are beginning to turn in your favor, you're met with another obstacle that places you two steps back in life. Some of the greatest disappointments can be avoided if hope is built upon the foundation of the Holy Spirit. You can't avoid circumstances by having hope, but you can avoid disappointment from unmet expectations by building hope in the right place.

It's difficult to see a loved one suffer. My cousin Ruth and her husband Jason went through a tough time a couple of years ago. In 2009 they found out they were expecting their second child. Their first child, Caleb, was a miracle from God. Having a second child was a dream come true. They decided to name him Joshua. They received bad news from their doctor. Joshua had a chromosome disorder, and it did not look good. It was bad enough that one of the doctors suggested terminating the pregnancy. Jason and Ruth refused.

As a family, we prayed for a healthy baby. I remember talking with Jason during Thanksgiving of 2009. On top of this struggle, Ruth and Jason were faced with the monumental task of starting a gym in Eden Prairie, MN. Jason was facing incredible pressure in two areas of his life. At one point in the conversation, he wondered how much a person could take.

It is a natural tendency to place our hope in the outcome of answered prayer. That's why we pray, right? We hope that God will hear our prayers and answer the desires of our heart. Family and friends gathered in prayer and hoped for the best outcome for Joshua. What set Jason and Ruth apart from other people is that they, too, hoped for the best outcome for baby Joshua, but they also built their hope and trust into the ability of a loving God to do whatever was best. They placed hope not only in the outcome of a good possibility, but also in the surety of God's character.

In March of 2010, baby Joshua was born and lived for six hours. Immediate family surrounded Jason and Ruth and shared the hours that Joshua spent on earth. Joshua spent his last moments in the arms of his earthly father before being transferred into the arms of his heavenly father. Placing hope in God's ability isn't a guarantee for a pain-free life. Jason and Ruth felt the deep pain of loss. Their hope in God's character helped them through the loss. He helped them heal and become an inspiration for many. Today, their business is thriving, their lives are influential, and they love others deeply. The hardest thing we go through can be the opportunity to place our hope on the foundation that will never crumble. If we get that right, the Holy Spirit will bring us through anything.

You don't always win; sometimes you simply endure. Hope is the substance that will help you get beyond what you have to go through. If you can apply hope to endure your season, you give the Holy Spirit the opportunity to bring you through.

Attitude is Everything

Hope is a choice. The choice is an easy one for a surrendered heart to make because hope is the action of surrender. Don't underestimate the power of choosing hope—or what you place your hope in! Your attitude will determine where you place your hope. My hope is built on the possibility of something better; it is founded on the character and abilities of God. I choose to put on the hope coat when I believe the Holy Spirit can work miracles in the middle of a mess. Some of life's seasons are chilly, and you will need the insulation hope provides to make it through. Before leaving your house every morning, don't forget to put on your hope coat!

CHAPTER THREE

GOD'S BEEN THERE BEFORE

I still remember the wrestling state semi-finals from twenty years ago. My opponent was Rick Jore from Watford. It was my first time qualifying for the semi-finals; he had won the state wrestling championship a few years earlier. I knew I was in for a tough match, but I was happy to be there. Prior to the match, I happened to meet Rick in passing and we wished each other good luck.

The match was fairly uneventful. He scored a takedown for two points. I scored a reversal for two points. He scored an escape for one point, and towards the end of the match scored three back points on me. The final score was 6-2. He would be moving on to the finals of the state championship (and would later win); I would move on to the consolation round.

I occasionally think about that match. When we spoke before the match, I said I was happy to have come this far. Qualifying for the semi-final round of the tournament meant I had already defeated many people. It was quite an achievement and completely new territory for me. I wonder how the match would have turned out if I had wrestled like I had been there before instead of wrestling like it was my first experience. The score might have turned out in my favor. It might not have. One thing would have been different: I would have wrestled with less to lose. I would have been less conservative and more aggressive.

I wonder what it would look like if we lived with faith in a God who *has* been there before. True faith is living life like you've been there before.

What is Faith?

Hebrews chapter 11:1 (NLT) defines faith:

"Faith is the confidence that what we hope for will actually happen; it gives us assurance about things we cannot see."

The people listed in Hebrews 11 lived life with aggressive faith. They experienced difficulties yet moved forward with an unwavering faith in God. Some conquered; others were imprisoned or stoned. Still they had faith in God that He would bring about His promises to them. They believed in His promises for this life and the next. True faith is living life like you've been there before. The only difference is that even if *you* haven't been in a situation before, God has. You can live like God has been there before.

This Seems Impossible

I went to college with a man who had his arms ripped off in a farming accident. Both arms were torn away from his body by a power take-off shaft connected to a running tractor. He easily could have died right there on the spot, but he made his way to the house to call 9-1-1. Somehow, he entered the house and used a pencil in his mouth to dial the number. After completing that call, he waited for the ambulance in the bathtub so he wouldn't stain the carpet with his blood. My mind probably wouldn't have been as collected as his.

Tragedy and trauma can cause us to feel like something's been ripped from us. In many cases panic replaces thought processes. Raw emotions can bring out the worst kind of perspective, and our faith feels like it's been stolen. Living by faith in a world of changing, brutal circumstances can feel impossible.

Take heart. With God, these things are possible.

We only learn to live by faith when we trust God to bring us through something. Trust and faith are siblings. Faith is the evidence of living like God's got it all under control. Trust is the foundation for giving room for God to operate.

If you happen to go through trials and have a few bad days in a row, don't think that God has abandoned you. Sometimes we feel that God doesn't love us anymore because we're going through a tough time. That's one of the favorite lies of our adversary. If we believe that God's love is missing during bad circumstances, we lose the ability to walk in faith. Because of God's incredible love for us, He gives us opportunity to build our faith upon the foundation of trust. The right perspective is what makes living by faith completely possible. God's been here before. He's got this.

What's Next?

The very moment you choose to believe God for something greater, **you'll be tested**. That's not always bad. It's an opportunity to test the commitment and allow the Holy

Spirit to strengthen it. My Grandpa Bachman tells about the moment he believed God for something greater in his life:

> *We were in Grand Forks on a Monday night. Watson Argue was the speaker at a packed high school auditorium. Towards the end of the service, local preachers were standing in the back watching for people to raise their hand. I thought, "I'm getting tired of my life. I've lived so rough, I want something different."*
>
> *I put up my hand and put it down really fast. A pastor saw me and walked right up to me and asked me if I wanted to give my heart to the Lord. And I said yes. It was the happiest day of my life. It felt like two hundred pounds dropped off of my shoulders. It felt so wonderful, it was wonderful, and it still is wonderful.*
>
> *When I gave my heart to the Lord, I had a friend of mine who went to grade school with me. If you saw him, you saw me. After I got saved, that next night on Tuesday was one of our nights that we'd go out and have a rip-roaring time.*
>
> *He came by all dressed up and asked, "What's the matter?" I told him I wasn't going out. He asked me why. I said I got saved.*
>
> *"What? What? Tell me again?"*
>
> *I told him I got saved. He said, "I've never heard anything so crazy."*
>
> *For an hour he tried to get me to go, and I told him, "Rueben, I'm done with that life."*
>
> *He said, "Why don't you just come out tonight and then go ahead and serve the Lord?" I knew if I went once, I'd be gone.*

Grandpa's decision to serve God changed the course of our family's life. Because of his commitment to stand by his decision, the generations that followed Grandpa have committed to following Christ.

The moment you decide to pursue additional education, start a business, train for ministry, or lose weight, you will be tested in the decision that you've made. Stand firm and believe that God inspired you to make that decision. He will bring you through the test and into the promise. Remember, He's been here before.

Why is it Worth It?

One of my biggest disappointments happened on Thanksgiving Day. We were to attend a football game between the Dallas Cowboys and the Minnesota Vikings. In order to get into the game, we had to meet the guy who had the tickets. We arrived at the gate and waited. Game time was drawing closer, and it was time for the kick-off. We were still waiting. The kick-off happened, and I could hear the crowd roaring with the excitement. I could see an entrance to the stadium and considered running for it just to catch a glimpse of the action. The guy never showed, and we lost access to the game. We didn't have the tickets that would provide us the way in.

Living without faith is like living without access to the greatest events in your life. Why wouldn't you give God a chance to prove that He's been there before? Why not give Him an opportunity to test and perfect your faith so He can give you access to your destiny? Why not live by faith to have great access to His presence? Don't be like Reuben. Grandpa George made a decision because he knew there was more to life than what he was experiencing. Reuben lived for what he saw and what he experienced. Grandpa George chose to live by his faith, and God gave him access to the greatest events in his life. Before he died, he witnessed his family follow his example in serving Jesus. Nothing else compared with that.

Aggressive surrender creates opportunity for strong faith. Living by faith gives way to unprecedented workings of the Holy Spirit in our lives. I am glad to know that an ounce of my faith can activate the entire weight of God's presence to move mountains and restore life. When it comes down to it, our act of faith is really just an exercise in watching God work. Belief is our ticket that enables us to come along for the ride.

CHAPTER FOUR

LISTEN UP

I hate hearing tests. I haven't passed one of them. I cover my lack of hearing by reading lips. Once you learn how to read people's words, you can hear what they are saying. People who are hard of hearing can say funny things. My Grandpa George and Uncle Willie both had hearing aids. Listening to them talk to each other on the CB Radio was a highlight. Because they couldn't hear very well, they couldn't always pick up on what the other was saying and disagreed with each other even when they were talking about the same thing.

Although this is not the case, hearing deficiencies can be mistaken for a lack of intelligence. Just because a person cannot hear, it doesn't mean that he or she lacks mental skills. Someone who is hard of hearing may appear to be out of it or disconnected from others. Perhaps the funniest part of impaired hearing is the random statement. It is usually the obvious statement that everyone has already been talking about. The person with the lack of hearing (or lack of attention, for that matter) may be thinking about the exact thing that everyone is talking about, but they may come up with their solutions after the conversation has moved on to the next point.

Having a hearing deficiency can make life difficult. Communication is missed and misinterpreted. Have you ever felt that you have a hearing impairment when it comes to hearing God? The impairment may not be with our ears, but our hearts.

Calibrating the Heart

I'm not strong in science. My favorite memories of school science class were Bunsen burners and field trips. Patience in scientific things is not my strength. However, one thing I enjoyed doing was calibrating the moisture in our wheat crop before harvest. Before harvesting a field, we measured the moisture content from a sample of the crop. If there was too much moisture, we either had to dry the entire crop (which cost money) or wait for dry weather to harvest. An entire crop of wheat will rot if it's stored wet. A poor calibration could cause a big catastrophe. A heart not calibrated to the voice of the Holy Spirit can create a lot of confusion. If you want to hear the voice of the Holy Spirit with clarity, consider these actions:

- <u>Know the condition of your heart.</u> The voice of the Holy Spirit can be distorted when we have an inaccurate assessment of our own hearts. The heart is not full of good intentions. It is unstable, unruly, and the source of everything that corrupts a person. Words from the Holy Spirit are not a *product* of a good human heart; they come *in spite of* the nature of the human heart. Knowing your heart's condition will help you recognize the need for total surrender.
- <u>Practice caring for people.</u> Put others first. Helping others reduces selfishness. You'll be able to hear the voice of the Holy Spirit clearly when you don't seek

credit for something. Caring for people becomes natural with practice.
- Understand what God cares about. Start with the Bible. It reveals who God cares for and what He likes to see in people. What moves God's heart is meant to move yours. Understanding God's heart does not mean that you alone have to fix the injustices of the world. It simply means that you're beginning to hear what His heart says. From there, all things are possbile.

Measure Twice, Cut Once

When you are listening for the voice of the Holy Spirit, remember the carpenter's motto: "Measure twice, cut once." Before you speak what you hear, make sure that your heart has been calibrated and your words are few. People make several common mistakes when learning to listen to the voice of the Holy Spirit:
- Speaking when they should have remained silent,
- Causing other people to stumble because of their personal revelations, and
- Coercing others to do something because they *have to* instead of helping them to *want to*

We'll all make many mistakes learning how to listen to the Holy Spirit. Before you speak, measure twice what will come out of your mouth. The moment of pause can save a lot of trouble.

Free Words

I've rarely heard the voice of God speak audibly, but I've heard the voice of God spoken directly into my heart through another person's words. Words are powerful—they can damage, create freedom, or soften the hardest heart towards the Holy Spirit.

My brother Ryan is five years younger than me, and both of us wrestled in high school. My senior year in wrestling didn't turn out very well. I lost a few times in the state wrestling tournament and failed to place. That spring just before graduation, Ryan and I were traveling to Grand Forks, ND. I told him that even though I had a lot of success during my wrestling career, I thought he would have more success because of his wrestling style. Those words aren't the easiest to say coming off of a major disappointment. I recognized that Ryan had a different approach to wrestling that created many possibilities. He is a thinker and a technician. He looks at the details. In many matches, the details are the difference between winning and losing.

Ryan went on to win four state championships in wrestling. He was also inducted into the National High School Hall of Fame in Stillwater, OK. It wasn't my words that helped him win championships. He had to go through difficult obstacles and win them by himself. But those words helped his confidence. In many cases, the most powerful words are those of encouragement. These are words that cost very little to say but carry incredible value.

Marketing the Heart of God

We are marketing agents for the content of our hearts. At some point, whatever is secret will be made public. What if the content of our hearts were the very words of the Holy Spirit? How could the lives of those around you become better by hearing words of life? Surrendered people are marketing agents for the intentions of God. They are reflectors of God's glory to a darkened world. They speak life because they hear clearly. Surrender to the Holy Spirit paradoxically makes them stronger!

This message can be understood and caught by others. It causes others to pause and think about God's intentions for their lives. Surrendered people campaign for hope. That's a message the whole world will listen to.

CHAPTER FIVE

MICROMANAGING THE HOLY SPIRIT

When someone believes that God IS, they give Him license to do what He thinks is best. True faith is not hinged upon God's ability; it's based on God's ingenuity. Faith creates access for God to work freely. God works things out for the good of those who believe in Him.

By faith my Dad and Mom sold the family farm and began a journey in missions work. For Dad, this decision was right but difficult because he loved farm life. Years earlier, my folks were part of a singing group called Bread of Life. They traveled across the country performing concerts in local churches. One of their songs was called "Whatever It Takes."[1] My Dad's part in this song was this:

Take my houses and lands,
Change my dreams and my plans,
For I'm placing my whole life in your hands.
And if you call me today,

---
[1] Lanny Wolfe

To a land far away,
Lord, I'll go and your will obey.

Years later the call to lands far away was answered as my parents followed God's call. They followed God's call because they believed who was calling them. It wasn't just about the call to go to another country; it was about following the one calling. They believed in God and His ability to order their steps. By faith they were willing to give up a farm and pursue a mission.

Their first stop was Costa Rica for language school. Learning a second language is difficult. Learning a second language while in midlife can feel impossible. Many missionaries went home after class in tears and deeply frustrated. Nonetheless, my parents stuck with it. Throughout Mexico and other countries in Central America, they had the opportunity to work with missionaries, and they led construction teams from the United States to build new churches. Those early years provided many new opportunities to learn and grow.

The next stage brought them stateside to work for Convoy of Hope. They traveled overseas, helped in community outreaches, and journeyed to disaster stricken areas. Mom helped start a gardening program. For four years, they ministered and did whatever was asked of them. During a transition period, they moved back to North Dakota to raise funds for their next assignment with Sustain Hope, a new organization within the Assemblies of God. The mission was sustainable living solutions in other countries. They began their work in 2010. Teaching in Bible schools, developing alternative cooking methods, and providing education for gardening consumed most of their time.

The fall of 2012 brought a challenge with it. Family circumstances, continuous travel, and a heavy schedule caused them to take a look at life. While feeling exhausted and depleted, they knew that they couldn't close up shop and simply retire. God's call was still on them and they were willing to follow. It just seemed like it took a lot more energy now. A new opportunity emerged. Substance-abuse recovery centers facilitated by Teen Challenge were seeking solutions of self-sufficiency. Many of these Teen Challenge centers were located throughout the world in places that could support sustained agriculture. Some centers had acres of grassland for cows; other locations were near bodies of water to raise tilapia. A few centers had large plots of land for vegetable gardens.

Dad and Mom traveled to a few centers and experienced a renewal of passion and energy. Part of that passion came from doing something they loved. Their experience on the farm was being used. Skills they hadn't used in years were now given the opportunity to flourish. Business plans were developed to sustain small farming endeavors, and gardening with purpose was implemented. What my parents had given up years ago was now being returned. I remember when the journey began in 1999 after the farm auction. What they sowed on the farm through generations of hard work was being returned to them in broken lives being rebuilt. Because they believe in who God is, God showed them what He could do.

I Want to Believe

Everyone wants to believe in something that can help them. Some people believe in the power of money to lift them from poverty. Some people believe in the strength of leadership to solve their problems. Others believe in themselves to create opportunities. These belief systems are based on systems that can fail. Everyone also wants to believe in something they can count on. They want to believe in something that shows the evidence first, but God operates differently. Our belief in Him has to be free from limitations for Him to work completely. Limited belief is like limited surrender. Neither of them will bring complete freedom.

We like to negotiate. If I do this, you'll do this. If you don't do this, I won't do this. God even makes deals. He demonstrated His ability to keep up His end of a deal throughout the history of the Old Testament. He's not afraid to negotiate with people either. But there's a way that's better than negotiating with God. That way is unlimited belief. If you have limited belief, you might think like this:

- We believe for God to answer our prayers in this way: fill in the blank.
- I think God will answer my prayers because I've done some good things.
- Because I prayed for this person's healing, I believe they will receive a good report from the doctor.
- I asked God to help us get out of debt through a miraculous donation.

All of these things are worthy of prayer. Healing is good. Wholeness is good. Debt-free living is good. Placing conditions on how God works is not. It doesn't take great faith to tell God what to do. It takes great faith to pray and get out of His way. Wait until the end so you can see what God meant to do. You can believe. Let God know what your heart desires and let Him work with it. Give Him time to accomplish the multiplication of your belief and obedience.

What Now?

Worry levels weaken when belief levels are strengthened. The conditions in your prayers will become less prevalent as you trust God's character more deeply. In your prayers, continue to be specific with God, just give Him the room to work in them. A frustration of mine is to be given something to do and then to be micromanaged on how to do it. I feel if you give me the project, you should trust me to complete it or not give it to me at all. This is how we ought to give God our belief to work in things. Either give Him our whole, unlimited belief with freedom to do anything, or don't give it to Him at all. Let your belief match the Holy Spirit's ability to operate. God is able to do anything we ask. Give Him the room to operate without limitation. That is the action of a true believer.

CHAPTER SIX

THE REBEL AND THE HEIR

Rebels are identified by their lack of submission to authority. Sometimes rebels have a cause; other times the authorities are right. At times, neither side is right, but the one with the most power is left standing. Rebellion begins when people see things differently than the authority. Misrepresentation is the birthplace of dissension. Rebels view authority as out of touch, controlling, or even oppressive.

Rebellion also creates martyrs. Some people are willing to give their life to overthrow a kingdom that ruins their lives. The problem with all rebellions is that there is no end to the cycle once it begins.

People tend to cheer for the underdog. It's nice to see evil empires toppled and monopolies broken up. Too much power causes corruption. But we can carry that same rebellion in our hearts when confronted with the action of complete, unconditional surrender.

The Identifier

In February of 2014, we buried my Grandpa Bachman. I identified with him in many ways. I grew up on a farm across the road from him. He was a farmer, my dad was a farmer, and I worked with them growing up. Grandpa was a hunter, drove snowmobiles, and loved Jesus. I identified with all of that. It wasn't just the bloodline that made me an heir; it was the identification I had with him that solidified it. I reflect my dad; he reflects his dad, and so on. There are common identifiers that give us the name of Bachman.

The differences between a rebel and an heir are minimal. Both care passionately about what they fight for. Both believe they are right. Both even care about other people who walk with them. The difference between a rebel and an heir is that one identifies with the heart of the Father. The other identifies only with his own heart.

An heir understands the heart of God in the middle of suffering. A rebel curses God because he thinks God should have done something about it. An heir realizes that pain and sorrow create an opportunity to give all of his life to God. A rebel recognizes authority only as long as things are fine and he is left alone. Once a rebel is asked to align his will to the heart of the king, his true nature comes out.

An heir struggles with the very same nature. Just being an heir does not make decisions of the will any easier. An heir realizes God's intent behind their suffering is meant for good. Suffering is their golden opportunity to overcome their inner rebellion. No one makes an heir kneel before God. Unconditional surrender to the work of the Holy Spirit gives an heir power to overcome his will to embrace God's will.

Living on Empty

Heirs choose to pour out their lives for the sake of God's purposes. The Holy Spirit can enable someone to do something this radical. Jason Streuble has poured out his life for God's purposes. Jason is a soil scientist and an ordained minister. His life's story took him through stops at Northwest University, Washington State University, staff positions at a local church, senior pastorate at another, and understudy to a local scientist. During the process of his preparation, Jason saw the hand of God engineering circumstances and providing provision for his family. One of his greatest influences came through the life of Bill Randolph at Northwest University, where Jason was studying for his degree in missions. Bill emphasized the idea of sustainable mission work geared towards meeting the physical needs of people through compassion ministry. This is when the idea of sustainability stuck in Jason's heart.

A devastating earthquake crushed Haiti in January 2010. Buildings were leveled, people were killed, and a new generation of orphans emerged within hours. Aid came to Haiti from all over the world, and Convoy of Hope was on the ground in response to the situation. Haiti would need time to rebuild. The problem with their rebuild was that the country was already used to other people providing aid and help. They had little opportunity or incentive to exercise their own ability and experience the dignity of a country being sustained by its own work. That was about to change. Jason Streuble joined Convoy of Hope in July of 2011. He soon secured a few nicknames such as "Dr. Dirt" and the "Sultan of Soil." He began work in Haiti shortly after his arrival with the focus of helping create food sustainability. God's hand in Jason's circumstances led him to this moment in time to help a country emerge out of devastation.

The first step began with education. To create sustainability, people need to possess the desire for change. Jason began working with a group of local farmers to build better crop production into their operation. With his knowledge and hands-on approach, Jason soon began to see increased yields. In addition to the increase in yields, the farmers had a market to sell their crops in Convoy of Hope's children's feeding program. It was a win-win. As of summer of 2014, over 3,500 farmers are on their way towards agricultural sustainability after going through the education program that Jason and his team created. These farmer's crops have produced over 1 million meals to help support the people of their country.

There are ways for vocational people who may be interested in participating in ministry to use their talents. Heirs follow God to the ends of the earth. They use their abilities to do what others think is impossible. Jason's experience has taught him to find ways to pour out what God has given him to use. He encourages others, "There's a reason that God has given you talents. Don't let anyone else tell you otherwise."

Weaken Your Personal Rebellion

Personal rebellion is subtle. It's the mindset that limits surrender towards the Holy Spirit and keeps us from fulfilling God's purposes. Personal rebellion keeps us from pouring out the talents that God has given us to change the world. Consider these steps to crush the rebellion:

- Maintain composure in the middle of the trouble. This composure is not just emotional composure. It's the composure that comes from trusting the Holy Spirit. Emotions are unstable and cannot be trusted. Your heart can be calm during turbulent times when following the lead of the Holy Spirit. Having good composure is developed by following the Holy Spirit. Following well begins with total trust.
- Try big things even when failure is possible. Preservation of our personal image strengthens personal rebellion. No one wants to look dumb in front of others. Heirs with Christ aren't afraid to try big things if the Holy Spirit leads them. Every failure is an opportunity to grow. Every success is an opportunity to give God glory. When you stop worrying about preserving your own image and start focusing on who you're becoming, personal rebellion loses power.
- Identify with the values of the Holy Spirit. The Holy Spirit is the reflection of Christ's life. He points to the work of the cross as His reason to be on earth. Without Jesus, there is no life. The Holy Spirit is here to convict the world of sin and to teach us all things. An heir identifies with the work of the Holy Spirit in their lives. They value what is important to God, and their lives are a reflection of Christ's life.
- Practice loving others. This is not possible through our own efforts because there are simply too many jerks in the world. It is only possible with the Holy Spirit. A rebel looks for people they identify with. An heir finds those who need identification with a savior.
- Ignite other people to pursue their callings. A movement of followers trumps a movement of rebels. Rebels fray because they ultimately have never learned to follow; followers become united to the

leader. If you want to crush your personal rebellion, help other people find their calling. Even if it costs you something, there's nothing like helping someone else become free from their own personal rebellion.

Don't Be Fooled

Not everyone who starts the race finishes. Not everyone is able to overcome the rebel tendencies inside of them. We don't finish what we start when we love our own lives to death. Beating the inner rebellion will be a battle as long as we live in this earthly tent. However, as long as we live in this body, we still have access to the empowering ability of the Holy Spirit. That is our hope. Live well in pursuing the Holy Spirit. Let the Holy Spirit shine a light into every area of your heart. With that light, it will be easy to determine if you are a rebel or an heir. If your heart is full of rebellious tendencies, the Holy Spirit can change that. Become the heir you were meant to be. Weaken the rebellion and enjoy the journey God takes you on.

CHAPTER SEVEN

DEFEATING THE DICTATOR

There's a dictator within us. He loves being king. He convinces strong people to become weak and tricks smart people into making dumb choices. He justifies immorality. The dictator is our will.

I know the power of the will. I have a strong one. I've learned (and I'm still learning) how to make it submissive to the will of the Holy Spirit. The choices I make based on natural feelings can keep me from reaching supernatural goals. When I choose spiritual obedience—at the expense of the dictator—I experience the Holy Spirit's direction and purpose.

I realized the power of fatigue my first semester in college. It happened in Omaha, NE, during a wrestling match. There was a moment in that match when I decided that a win just wasn't worth the fatigue I was feeling. My coach saw that moment too. When I came off of the mat after suffering a narrow defeat, he confronted me and told me that I should have won that match. He recognized the difference in me the moment I gave into fatigue. My coach was absolutely right. My body convinced my mind that it was too tired to complete the job. I believed my body, and it caused me to lose a match I should have won.

The little dictator in us convinces us that transformation through the Holy Spirit is not worth the cost. The dictator uses fatigue to make us listen to how we feel, rather than focus on who we are becoming.

The Path of Least Resistance

Our will persuades us to choose the path of least resistance. It's the path that's wide, flat, and easy to walk. It's not easy to choose the right way when the will is crying about how hard something is. The Holy Spirit will not demand that you choose His way. We have to *want* the things that the Holy Spirit values if we want to change the world. The Holy Spirit helps us in our weaknesses and provides direction for difficult choices. He is there to direct and provide but makes no demands on us. We get to intentionally decide upon our true surrender.

Helping hurts when a person loses their dignity through accepting relief (food, water, clothing, money) with little direction towards personal transformation and empowerment. At some point, if mercy does not pave the way for empowerment, recipients of mercy begin to expect—and sometimes demand—relief without growing into their ability to provide for themselves.

It is a blessing to help others. It becomes a curse when the people being helped begin to lean on the helper for things that they can do themselves. That's why the Holy Spirit will not do anything for us that we are not first willing to surrender. To overcome the power of the dictator will, we need to learn the path the Holy Spirit wants us to take.

We can follow the Holy Spirit effectively when we are willing to count the cost. Following the Holy Spirit is simple but demanding. The Holy Spirit is not bossy; He's consistent in displaying truth. The demanding part comes from consistently telling the little dictator to be quiet. It's a constant battle with a wayward will, but it's one that can be overcome by the work of the Holy Spirit in us. You may be closest to a checkpoint in your journey with the Holy Spirit when you're most fatigued. Just like that wrestling match that I lost, you'll face similar situations in life when you feel that following the Holy Spirit to conclusion just isn't worth it. The moment you feel that way, just remember that you are close to a checkpoint. Keep moving.

Indicators that Your Will is Alive

You'll know when your dictator is growing stronger when you feel:

- <u>Impatience with a situation</u>. Things aren't moving fast enough. Circumstances are not coming together and people are moving slowly. The moment you feel impatient, you need to pause and reflect where that motivation is coming from. Even if it's something good that isn't happening fast enough, impatience can derail the process and cause harm. Remember, rash decisions can wreck an entire process.
- <u>Increasing frustration</u>. This is when you begin to look at people differently. People are the problem; they are impeding the process of greatness. The Holy Spirit may be on the verge of giving you divine instruction. Don't forfeit a great learning opportunity by blaming someone for holding you back. God is never stopped by anyone; He always works through the situation.

- **Rising stress levels.** You lose sleep and gain weight. There are few advantages to living in the stress of a moment. Stress increases when we try to figure out the situation for ourselves. Stress rises when we take things upon ourselves that are not ours to solve. Through our stress, we could be doing a job that we are not meant or equipped to do. Stress is the result of misplaced trust.

These indicators are gauges to be monitored. I once owned an old Nissan Sentra. Every time I filled up the car with gas, I had to add a quart of oil. The oil issue in my car was a result of an indicator that wasn't addressed. My engine overheated during a short trip in town, and I did not stop to let it cool down. I hurried to make it to my destination and in the process, caused harm to the motor. If we don't listen to the indicators in our lives, we may give the little dictator control over our lives and separate us from the Holy Spirit's influence.

There Is Hope

Sometimes it may feel like we are losing the battle with our will. It's a normal feeling. We can overcome our natural tendencies when we decide to follow the Holy Spirit. The Holy Spirit will not force our decision. He will work with our *want-to* and make us everything He wants us to be. We can unseat the little dictator from power every single day if we intentionally make a choice to listen to the Holy Spirit.

Following the Holy Spirit is like learning how to let Him drive. Growing up in the mid-seventies, we didn't have modern rules concerning car seats and seat belts. My car seat faced forward and was in the front seat. On one trip with my parents, I decided that I wanted to drive. The obvious step was to grab the steering wheel, which I did. As a toddler, the first time is cute. "No-no," my dad said. Taking my hand off of the wheel, he put it in my lap. No sooner than he did that, I reached over and grabbed the steering wheel once again. The no-no's turned into slapped hands and running tears as I refused to listen. I don't know how long this cycle lasted but my folks tell this story with great enthusiasm while laughing and laughing. Even though I wanted to drive the car, I wasn't ready yet. I had to learn that listening to my dad was safest for the entire family.

Our spirit grows stronger by listening. Listening is an act of focus. Pausing is an act of stillness. We can listen to the Holy Spirit when we practice focusing and pausing. We may not hear the Holy Spirit every time we pause or focus, but we are creating a place for Him to work in us. That space in our hearts will be the amplifier for His voice to be heard.

We can steward our bodies. This isn't just an act of fitness; it's an act of worship. The little dictator causes the most trouble when we've not had enough sleep. He wreaks havoc when we're hungry. He causes us to indulge in laziness when we don't move. One of the best ways (and definitely least desirable) to quiet the little dictator is fasting. Nothing reveals issues more quickly than abstaining from food for the purpose of spiritual development. Fasting is like a truth serum: it clears away the fuzziness and causes us to realize what really motivates us.

We can also serve others. Being aware of other people's needs quiets the voice of the will. The little dictator loses influence when we love other people. What better way to demonstrate the heart of Jesus than to serve and help another person?

We don't have to follow the dictator. He doesn't have to convince us that the easy way is better. We don't have to become cowards and submit to fatigue. The Holy Spirit will lead us to the best place. It's going to take some effort. It's going to be hard. But it's going to be worth it. That's something no dictator has ever been able to deliver.

CHAPTER EIGHT

JAILBREAK

Forgiving is hard to do. I know when people have left pieces of themselves in broken situations. You can tell what a person thinks about by what they talk about. Sometime their words reveal the journey not yet taken towards total forgiveness.

Matthew West wrote a song about a lady named Renae who lost her child in a car accident caused by a drunk driver. To overcome this tragedy, Renae decided to help others realize the dangers of drunk driving. She shared her story with thousands of people nationwide. As she toured the country with her message, she realized that there was something missing. There was an element of that story yet to be written. God was working on her heart to forgive the man who had taken the life of her child. She reached out to Eric, the man who had killed her daughter, and extended forgiveness to him. Her family soon followed her lead. For the final step, Renae approached the courts about reducing Eric's sentence. The courts cut Eric's prison term in half and released him in 2012.

Releasing Me

That story reflects a surrendered life. How else could someone who had lost so much be able to let go of so much more? Renae had every right to be angry. Instead, she broke out of the prison of unforgiveness. When someone has wronged me, I tend to hope that something bad happens to them. I'm sure you don't entertain those thoughts. You've probably never hoped for that other person to have a flat tire on their way to work or to be overdrawn at the end of the month.

I've come to realize that every time I hope for something bad to happen to my offender, I return to prison. The jail cell has no use except to contain hurt. Nothing can be done behind bars. There's no way to communicate with the outside world. You miss connecting with the purpose of life. There's certainly no freedom in the middle of that little cell. The moment I forgive is the moment I break out of jail. The pieces of me that were broken become repaired by the work of the Holy Spirit. I can choose to remain bitterly broken, or I can trust the work of the Holy Spirit by releasing the outcome into His hands.

Being Close to the Enemy

One of the greatest acts of surrender is to trust God with your enemies. Your enemies are those who are against you in some way:
- People who disagree with you
- People who have hurt you
- People who betray you
- People who undermine or limit you

PARADOX · 45

- People who are jealous of you

How do I trust God with my enemies? These definitions are tame. Obviously, people have done much worse. The problem in measuring the fruit of hate and murder is that sometimes we forget the seed it comes from.

Rose Mapendo is a walking reflection of God's grace and forgiveness. As a Congolese refugee, she was forced to watch the murder of her husband. This is her story:

I wanted to share my story. Always when I share with people my story, what happened, I wish I can be the last one who is suffering. Refugees are normal people like us, like you and like me. It is someone who lost everything in one minute and found themselves in a death camp. When my husband died, was just the time I found out I was pregnant. I was so scared. Every end of the day was an end of a life. Because they came and chose some friends and took outside and killed. And every day we were thinking "Will we be the next?"

I gave birth to twins. It was dark. No light. I tried to find something clean we can cut the umbilical cord with, but we can't find. Everything was dirty. After we cut the umbilical cord, we cannot find something to tie to stop the bleeding. I took something from my hair and I tied it.

I believe that if I share my story, others may feel inspired to help those in need. And I know the importance of help, even if it's just a small cup of cold water from someone. I help refugees that come to the United States. My prayer to God, I wish everyone to be free. Because I believe when you don't forgive others, you keep building a hell for yourself.

After I gave birth to the twins in prison, I thought, what will save my babies' lives? I decided; let me name my children after the army commanders. Maybe it would

> *save their lives, they wouldn't be killed. In Kasai culture, naming your child after someone means you love them. It was not easy for me because these were the people who had killed the father of my children. But I asked God to help me forgive my captors who thought I was their enemy. And when I forgave them, I felt like somebody had lifted a big stone off of me.*
>
> *Peace filled my heart.*
>
> *I forgave.*
>
> *Even now, I forgive.*
>
> *There are so many people who think vengeance is the solution. But to me, vengeance is not the answer. I think about the future, the next generation. I think unity and reconciliation are needed for people to have peace.*[2]

Rose is an advocate for survivors of war, especially women and children. You can be an advocate for survivors when you forgive the worst of your enemies.

At some point, you'll need to leave the cell of unforgiveness. The only way to exit that cell is to enter love for your enemy. Entering into love for your enemy is an act of the will that surrenders fate into the hands of God. Revenge is not the answer. When you truly forgive someone, you gain a perspective of who they are and why they act the way they do. Rose said that she wishes she could be the last person to suffer. Real love wishes for no one to suffer but for all to become healed and whole. Real love enables you to hear the hurt of your enemy's heart. Real love causes you to pray for them.

---

[2] Video.pbs.org/video/2207180747/

Wise as a Snake

A benefit from total forgiveness is wisdom. There's nothing like a good old-fashioned heartbreak to teach the art of drawing boundaries. Don't build walls. Walls separate and isolate. Boundaries are defined roles to preserve friendships and cause enemies to be at peace with you. With boundaries, you never have to worry about trying to please someone for their approval. Trying to please someone may have caused your heartache in the first place. When you embrace God's intention of creating you in His image, you stop trying to please everyone. Becoming healed also creates boundaries that stop the bleeding from old wounds.

Wisdom creates the opportunity to totally trust God. With wisdom, you don't have to worry about being wrong or hurting someone else. Wisdom is the mind of God for life. Being a whole person is possible when the mind of God helps to define confusing situations. A whole person understands that the Holy Spirit is working in them, through them, and around them. While they may suffer for a moment, God is working in them a movement of grace and power. A whole person realizes that their enemies are not really their enemies. Enemies are broken people, and they need a special kind of love. You might be the only person on earth that can give them that kind of love. When you become a whole person through forgiveness, you become a person that is at peace.

CHAPTER NINE

RELENTLESS PURSUIT

No one likes a bully. During my 7th grade year, I was bullied. It was not a happy season. At eighty-five pounds, there wasn't much I could do to deter the two-hundred-pound-plus guy from bugging me. I tried to stay out of his way. Later on, as I grew and had success on the wrestling team, he left me alone.

My wife Natalie also experienced bullying. She tried to avoid confrontation until one day she had enough. That day, the bully was up to his usual shenanigans when Natalie grabbed him by his collar and slammed him against the locker. Holding her fist in his face, she told him that if he continued to bother her, he would get to know her fist very well. He didn't cause her any more trouble.

The tyrant bullying us is our own desire. Have you ever done something that you wish you hadn't? Being bullied by selfish desire is a lack of freedom. During a mission internship, I lived in a home where the mother had recently returned from rehab. She did well the first couple of weeks home but began to slip back into her drug addiction. Her behavior changed, and items in the house disappeared, my camera included. Drug use is a powerful tyrant. I don't know if she ever conquered that demon or not. All I know is that I saw firsthand how destructive the inner tyrant can be.

What Does Freedom Look Like?

Some define freedom as doing whatever you want whenever you want to do it. Others define freedom as doing things they want to do as long as it doesn't hurt other people. I define freedom as the ability to relentlessly pursue the purposes of God. This relentless pursuit is a benefit that comes from a surrendered life.

Shortly before Jesus went back to Heaven, He told Peter he would be bound up and directed where to go. That didn't sound like the freedom that Christ died for. It sounded like Peter was bound to a dull and meaningless existence, being told by others what to do. Actually, Jesus was describing the freedom Peter would experience by finally surrendering to the Holy Spirit. Peter struggled with surrender because of his strong personality. He would learn that the closer people get to the heart of God, the more defined their focus becomes and the more their courage rises to meet the task.

True freedom looks like the people who are content with what they have, who no longer fear the future, who care for someone in need. True freedom looks like the people who mimic the life of Christ on this earth.

- **Contentment** is being satisfied with what you have while pursuing the purposes God has placed in your heart. Contentment is the inner assurance that God will provide what you need.
- **Bravery** during uncertainty is a characteristic of the Holy Spirit's freedom. Bravery creates assurance of God's ability to control all things. People who are

brave toward the future steward their lives well. Brave people pursue God's destiny and purpose.
- **Caring** for others creates freedom from selfishness. Entering the mess of human relationships is difficult, inconvenient, and costly. However, the cost of selfishness compounds during a lifetime, causing greater cost than most are willing to pay. Caring for others removes the tyrant of selfish thinking and replaces it with love towards others.

Real freedom is expressed by imitating Christ's life with our own. Jesus lived with high purpose; it motivated Him to listen for the Father's direction. Listening precedes liberty. Obedience provides opportunity. Experiencing the freedom from individual tyranny is worth the price of following Jesus.

What's the Alternative?

Denial is an alternative. Most people will live their lives fulfilling the passions and desires of their inner selves (tyrant) while never experiencing the freedom of fulfilling God's desires. They will consider themselves free because they can do what they want, when they want to. Freedom to them will look like just a little bit more: earning a bit more money, gaining another level of prestige, or building another creation. This type of tyranny is hard to break away from because we *still feel like we are in control*. We're really not. We're just chasing harder after things that fade, rust, and become corrupted.

What Will I Need to Do for Freedom?

For your freedom, you'll need to do the hardest thing that God asks you. For a rich young leader, it was selling his possessions to the poor. For a gang member, it was giving up the perks of leadership to follow Christ. For a farmer, it was selling the farm to become a missionary. For these real-life people, their obedience was the doorway to their freedom. Some chose freedom; others chose their possessions. What act of obedience will be the doorway to your freedom? Consider this: whatever you surrender in your life creates access for the Holy Spirit to work inside of you. When the Holy Spirit has greater influence in our lives, true freedom emerges. The Holy Spirit provides true freedom. Other kinds of freedom are simply illusions.

Living in a New Reality

Once you live in the Holy Spirit's freedom, you'll understand that your life is meant to be poured out, not contained. You can understand the purposes of God for your generation. You'll experience liberty to pursue the callings of God. You'll be able to pursue God's purposes without restraint. You won't be indecisive, confused, or hesitant. You'll be fulfilled, full of peace, and motivated by joy.

At a Convoy of Hope outreach in Kenosha, Wisconsin, I spoke with a volunteer who was serving at the event. That morning, her heart was not into serving and she had contemplated staying home. As she greeted our guests entering the site, she was overwhelmed with compassion and convicted by her own selfishness. She had been a prisoner of her own selfishness. That day, she was liberated through serving others. With tears in her eyes, she expressed her gratitude of being able to participate and help make a difference.

The new reality of freedom will impact you in ways you cannot imagine. The cost of living in this new reality is the price of your obedience. The yoke that Jesus gives us is not heavy or burdensome. With your obedience, the Holy Spirit has an avenue to pour out His power and passion equal to your task.

The Blessing of Freedom

The inaugural address of Jesus Christ from the Gospel of Luke says:

"The Spirit of the Lord is upon me, because he has anointed me to proclaim good news to the poor. He has sent me to <u>proclaim liberty to the captives</u> and recovering of sight to the blind, to <u>set at liberty those who are oppressed.</u>" Luke 4:18 (ESV)

When you proclaim liberty to oppressed people, it is backed up by the power of the Holy Spirit working through you. The blessing of following God's instruction and seeing Him work miracles through you is true freedom. Those who walk in freedom now have opportunities to create freedom for others. Not only do I benefit from all the blessings of being truly free, now I can help others experience their freedom as well. You can, too.

CHAPTER TEN

INDESTRUCTIBLE

Wolverine is one of my favorite superheroes. He is indestructible, he has healing qualities that support a metal-infused skeleton, and his nasty attitude helps him defeat the bad guys. He can't sleep very well, though. He often has nightmares from his past. His memory has been partially wiped out, and he has trouble getting close to people. The broken sleep is probably a factor in his overall grumpiness.

He actually has a lot of issues. Most of them can be covered up in the middle of battle with the enemy. However, the enemy can use Wolverine's memories against him. In some cases, Wolverine is sidetracked while pursuing the meaning of his life and forgets his current purpose. In other cases, his trouble connecting with people makes it easy for him to walk away from his team and the people who care about him. Internal issues derail the greatest potential. Internal brokenness can be healed by the work of the Holy Spirit and used for helping other people become healed.

A Broken Body, an Indestructible Spirit

Over forty years ago, a young woman was crippled in a diving accident. At the prime of her life, she broke her neck while diving in a shallow part of a lake. She was paralyzed. She had to learn how to cope with this new reality. Paralysis robbed her of dignity since others now had to assist her with eating, dressing, and using the restroom. She could have given up hope. Instead, she used her brokenness to bring healing to millions. Joni Eareckson Tada has shared her experience with the world. She decided to use her pain for purpose and has helped facilitate public policy for people with disabilities. Millions have listened to her radio program, *Joni and Friends*. Her ministry, Wheels for the World, collects wheelchairs for people with disabilities in foreign countries. The Wounded Warriors retreat offers hope for families with wounded veterans returning from service. None of this would have happened if she had let the destruction of her physical body destroy the integrity of her spirit. One of the greatest benefits of surrendering to the complete work of the Holy Spirit is the ability to become indestructible.

Coping with Loss

Few people enjoy being sick. Multiple generations have been looking for the secret to youth, the secret to wholeness, and the secret to living beyond death. Religions and habits have been passed down in hopes that someone will, someday, be able to find a cure for the sickness that ails humanity. This cause, trying to make what is temporary eternal, is futile. People who look to live forever on earth miss the point. Our bodies won't live forever, but our spirits will.

Realizing this concept might be one of the hardest struggles of all in unconditional surrender. We can do little about the time appointed for all of us to die. We can, however, create a space for the Holy Spirit to teach us about coping with loss and realizing the greater gain that waits in eternity. God does heal. We don't have to be afraid of sickness that might kill us. God is intentional about healing the part of our lives that will live forever. We can be like Wolverine (tough on the outside, broken on the inside), or we can be like Joni (whole in the middle of brokenness) and learn how to use any loss for the healing of our spirits.

The benefit of unconditional surrender is the ability to deal with loss in a healthy way. Loss may cripple our outward appearance or destroy a closely held relationship. Loss has never been God's original plan for humanity. Loss is the by-product of free will. Sometimes we'll experience loss; other times we won't. What we can always experience—through surrender—is the healing that God provides for the deepest part of our soul.

Pain: the Great Distractor

It doesn't matter how tough you are, pain causes poor decisions. The secret is to work through pain and allow the Holy Spirit to fill the holes caused by trauma. Keep in mind these things when dealing with pain:
- God has not abandoned you. When Jesus died on the cross, God turned His back upon the sin that Jesus became. Since Jesus became sin for us, God will not turn His back on us.

- **God will give you strength.** In every situation of pain, God will provide grace. Accepting grace is difficult in the middle of pain because it doesn't eliminate the issue. Grace simply helps you get through the issue. God did not rescue Jesus from the cross. We wished for a rescue, but God meant it for a resurrection. God will give you grace to make it through the pain.
- **God will give you wisdom.** There are opportunities to express wisdom in the middle of chaos. During these trying times, wisdom can be the nugget of information you need for the next step. Wisdom isn't always what we want, but it is always what we need.
- **God's love will remove fear.** Painful times are tough because they are uncertain. Fear is strong in times of struggle when the outcome is unclear. God's love will help you realize that everything works together for your good. God's love is consistent towards you. When you return God's love back to Him, there is no room for blame.

If you remember these things, you can get through pain while keeping your inner-self intact. Don't let pain distract you from becoming indestructible in spirit. The Holy Spirit will empower you to get through any situation. Trust Him with the trouble.

Constant Healing

Justin Werven, son of Gordie and Linda Werven, Cavalier, appears to be a healthy, normal, first grader. Unfortunately, this is not so in Justin's case. From the time he was two months until eleven months old, he is in and out of the Cavalier Clinic and Pembina County Memorial Hospital.

A couple of weeks before his first birthday, Justin was admitted into the United Hospital in Grand Forks. There Justin would be diagnosed with asthma.

Less than five months later Justin would once again be placed in United Hospital and spend another month there. While there, Justin went into Respiratory Arrest and spent three days on a respirator. Justin was now stable, but over the next couple of months showed no improvement. Because of this, Gordie and Linda looked into sending him some place that specialized in asthma.

Six months after Justin was released from United Hospital, now two years old, he was sent to National Jewish Hospital in Denver, Colorado. He would spend two more months in this hospital. Justin would only be in the hospital two times in 1984.

Justin seemed to be doing pretty well. Then, in May of 1988, his parents noticed he was having problems breathing. This time they were sent to a specialist in Fargo. After doing all they could, they sent Justin, once again, down to National Jewish Hospital. That was this past September.[3]

This time doctors found that a portion of the left lung was permanently damaged. Not only was he a severe asthmatic, but he also had a restrictive/obstruction disease of the lungs — so rare that they cannot put a name on it at this time.

---

[3] Excerpt of this article taken from the Cavalier Chronicle newspaper, April 4th, 1989.

> *This disease causes his lungs to function only 50 to 60 percent. Since they do not know much about this disease they cannot give Justin or his parents a prognosis.*

A few years ago, during a church service, James Maloney prayed for Justin. James didn't even say much of a prayer before Justin began coughing and coughing. It was like Justin was coughing the oxygen out of his lungs, and in one moment, he took the deepest breath he had ever taken.

He was healed.

In the coming months, Justin went off of his medication with the thought, "Lord, either you're going to heal me or you're going to kill me." That was back in 2009. Years later, Justin is doing well. He knew he was healed because of the breath he could take. Being indestructible is realized by each breath we take. Inner indestructibility is completely possible with an unwavering surrender to the Holy Spirit's work and trust in His methods.

James Maloney's methods of praying for Justin didn't heal Justin. The credit belonged to Jesus. James was joking around when God healed Justin. You can watch the video, "Justin Gets Prayed For" on YouTube.[4] The Holy Spirit might work in ways you least expect. You have to give Him room to work and realize that through His work we become indestructible. Even though our outer bodies waste away day by day, our inner selves are being renewed day by day.

You can experience constant healing by doing these things:

- <u>Don't base your destination upon your circumstances.</u> The pain you are going through now is not a death sentence to destiny. Circumstances are

---

[4] https://www.youtube.com/watch?v=_3La0Ow-YpQ

poor measuring tools. Faith in the Holy Spirit helps you see *through* the circumstances and identify purpose.

- Follow the peace. No matter what, listen to the voice of the Holy Spirit as He guides you through painful times. If you listen to the pain, you'll make a decision based on blindness. If you listen to the Holy Spirit, you'll get to the destination God intends.
- Let the Holy Spirit fuel your spirit. He will provide the strength, energy, and purpose to get up during the darkest hour. Trust Him and lean upon Him. However, if you blame Him for the troubles you're in, you can't take full advantage of His work in you. Blame creates distrust. Trust is the only thing that will get you through.

On a side note, Justin recently completed a marathon as an act of faith, partnering with God in his healing.

You can become indestructible, not through willpower, but through the Holy Spirit's power. Give God the opportunity to heal and restore your brokenness and watch Him redeem the situation. You may experience brokenness again, but this time you've got healing attributes that will help you walk again.

CHAPTER ELEVEN

SAME OLD RUT?

My friend Matt had a big Ford pickup that was perfect for the off-road trails. One day we went for a ride and got stuck in the snow. It didn't look bad until we realized that the U-joint on the front drive shaft connected to the four-wheel drive was broken. The only thing powering the truck was the rear wheels. With little weight on the back end, the wheels spun in the snow. We were done. We walked back to Matt's house and told his dad the truck was stuck. We didn't tell him that the truck was broken before we left him in the field to walk to the truck. After Matt's dad came home (by walking because we didn't have cell phones back then), I'm glad we're still alive.

If the Ford had all of the parts working properly, it would have been no problem to back out of the rut to get back on solid ground. It only took one little, broken U-joint to keep the truck in the rut and out of commission. If you lack the power or leverage to get out of the rut, you're stuck until someone helps you out. It can be the smallest things that keep you in the rut and from experiencing great change in your life.

Living Out of the Ruts

Living a surrendered life helps you deal with broken seasons of life. Everything has purpose when you live in unconditional surrender. With surrender, seasons have a beginning, an end, and a purpose. They don't have to feel like unending ruts.

Rich Dixon could have lived in a rut for the rest of his life, and no one would have blamed him. Years ago, he fell off a ladder and broke his neck. He was paralyzed from the chest down and soon gave up hope. For many years, Rich struggled with finding purpose to live. One day, Rich changed his thinking and decided to do something about his condition. He began to climb out of the rut, to start living. With the use of his arms, he began using a hand-pedal bike to move himself around. As he worked on increasing the distance of his rides, something happened inside of him. The Holy Spirit helped Rich realize a greater purpose.

He decided to ride across the country and share his story of hope. On one of those rides, he rode from Minnesota to the Gulf of Mexico. Along the way, he shared his overcoming story with churches, civic groups, and schools. God redeemed Rich's situation. Rich didn't live in the rut; he lived in the moment. It all began when Rich stopped feeling sorry for himself and began to look for the possibilities that God was giving him. Surrendering to the Holy Spirit helps us get out of the ruts and into real life.

Good Things Happen

If you've ever wanted to change how you act, respond, and think, you might want to consider the benefits of complete surrender.

- Surrender changes the way we respond. We respond differently when we know the outcome is sure. Everyone faces an uncertain future. Even when living in surrender, we don't know how circumstance will play out. However, we can be sure that the outcome is taken care of. When we trust the Holy Spirit's work, we know that all things work for good.
- Surrender changes the way we think. Our brains have ruts in them. They are called habits. Certain situations can trigger us to react in learned behaviors. Surrendered living helps us re-groove the thinking patterns in our minds to reflect the thought processes of God. Through the Holy Spirit, we can learn the ways that God operates. We do this by becoming better followers.
- Surrender provides a different perspective. Vision is increased with trust. The more I trust the Holy Spirit, the more I can see through the situation into God's purpose. Trusting the Holy Spirit helps me see a situation without the negative influence of my unstable emotions. When I am unafraid of loss, I can clearly see the work of the Holy Spirit. My perspective becomes aligned with the purposes of God.
- Surrender changes my actions. My mind, soul, and vision become different through surrender. When that foundation is reset, my actions reflect

the change. I learn how to think differently, see differently, and trust the Holy Spirit. All of these internal changes are reflected in the external expression of my actions. When things change, mentally and emotionally, you can be sure that your actions will reflect the new groove of thinking.

Learning Transformation

Transformation doesn't happen in a moment. Transformation is a movement facilitated by the moment when we align our will to the Holy Spirit. Learning how to be transformed can be like learning how to drive in another climate. Take snow for instance. If you've never driven in snow, remember these lessons if you ever drive up north:

1. Spinning your wheels does not help. Spinning your wheels creates ice under your tires. Ice is not known for traction. The less you spin, the more you can travel. Chill out with the gas pedal.
2. Drive as if you have no brakes. Begin slowing down for intersections way before you think you need to. Give consideration to other people who forget that snow is slippery.
3. If you get stuck in a little bit of snow, back up. You've already created a trail in the snow; use it by backing straight up. When you've given yourself some distance, you can attempt to drive forward again. Without spinning your wheels of course.
4. If you get stuck in deep snow, I hope you have a shovel or a friend with a truck. Hopefully they will have a rope.

Learning transformation is like driving in the snow. We may not be used to it, but with some help we can learn how to drive through it. The measure of transformation is not always the destination. It is movement. If you are moving, that means the Holy Spirit can work with you. If you think you've arrived, you'll probably stay in the rut you've created.

Don't Get Stuck

As you emerge from old ruts and old ways of thinking, be encouraged by the little things. Don't be discouraged if it takes some time to break old habits and negative mindsets. God is patient with your development. He's given you the Holy Spirit as power, inspiration, and teacher. Transformation, through surrender, is still facilitated by the Holy Spirit. It is simply our responsibility to follow where He leads. Let Him work out the details and the outcome. Don't get distracted by an apparent lack of progress. When God works, He does everything well. He's working a masterpiece inside of you.

CHAPTER TWELVE

THE RIGHT PERSPECTIVE

Woulda, shouda, coulda are words of those who view life through the rearview mirror. Surrendered people don't look back. Maintaining a consistent forward view is a benefit of a surrendered heart.

The 1998 Minnesota Vikings football team had great expectations leading up to the playoffs. During the regular season, they built a 15-1 record. On Thanksgiving Day, they played a game against the Dallas Cowboys. I almost had the opportunity to attend that game in person, but it didn't work out. Nonetheless, I was interested in the team up north and wondered how far they would go in the playoffs. For many years, the Vikings were notorious for teasing their fans with the hope of a championship only to blow it in a big game. They were the losers of four Super Bowls in previous years. The 1998 season held promise for a championship. In other years, every team that had won 15 games in the regular season went on to win the Super Bowl.

During the regular season, the offense put up the most points to date in the NFL. The quarterback to wide receiver combination produced numerous touchdowns. Even the defense played well, limiting opposing teams. This team was a machine running on all cylinders. Their opponent for the NFC

Championship game was the Atlanta Falcons, who were having a good year of their own. At 14-2, they were a quality team. Minnesota went into halftime leading 20-14. During the third and fourth quarter, the teams battled it out and ended with a tie at the end of regulation. They were going to overtime. The first score would win the game. For an offense that was productive all year long, it all fell apart in overtime. For whatever reason, the two times that Minnesota had possession, they failed to score, and Atlanta kicked a field goal to win the game, reserving their spot in the Super Bowl.

I remember watching that game and being disappointed for the Vikings and their fans. I also remember thinking during the overtime period that the Vikings were playing not to lose. There's a difference between playing to win and playing to avoid a loss. It seemed to me they were doing the latter. It looked like the pressure of previous failures were weighing the team down. Whether or not they were thinking those thoughts in the huddle, I bet there were fans thinking, "Here we go again."

We're meant to view life through the front windshield. A good perspective provides accuracy in navigating life's roadblocks and potholes. Memories of past failures may place pressure on attempts of success. The memories of the past only gain significance if they outweigh forward perspective.

Changing the Meaning

Pain is a four-letter word. Few people choose to experience pain; most spend their lives trying to avoid future pain. There's nothing fun about pain. Pain can also be very intimidating when viewed in a rearview mirror. The movie *Jurassic Park* is a great example of viewing pain a rearview mirror. In one scene, a T-Rex is pursuing a vehicle. When the camera pans to the side mirror, the characters see the reflection of a dinosaur in hot pursuit. Previous pain in our lives can look like that. It's something that we never wish to experience again.

What if we had a different perspective of pain we've experienced? How would perspective change if that pain was completely surrendered to the Holy Spirit? I think the perspective of pain would change dramatically. At some point, we have to stop being afraid of the dinosaur. It's in the past and extinct. Pain experienced in the past can be memorized and cripple future growth. The memory of what we experienced shapes the way we interpret current happenings. Someone who has good intentions for us can be viewed as harmful or dangerous through the lens of pain. The lens of pain can cause severe distortions of reality.

I began wearing glasses in the eighth grade. The eye doctor went through the normal testing procedure with lights, puffs of air, and a monstrosity of an eye machine. The testing was meant to help sharpen my perspective with the correct lenses. It worked. The moment I emerged from the eye clinic, I saw details that I hadn't seen before. The trees actually had singular leaves. They weren't just masses of green. Words in the distance meant something to me. I could read them. Can you imagine what might have happened if I had not gone through the testing of the eye exam?

"This has got to be the dumbest thing I have ever experienced!" I kicked over the table next to the chair as I got up to leave. "Who shines a light into someone's eye?" As I tipped over the lens machine, I yelled, "The next time I want my eye dried out with air, I'll ride a roller coaster!"

None of that stuff happened, of course. But some of that stuff does happen when we go through pain. We act crazy, and the doctor is reviled for trying to fix something. God doesn't stop bad things from happening because of other people's free will. What He can do is redeem the pain for good and provide perspective in healing.

Failure is not Final

Regret is a horrible energy source for motivation. I've driven machines since I was nine years old. Growing up on a farm provides many opportunities for driving failure. Consider a few of my own:

- Breaking the frame of a snowmobile after flying over a ramp
- Rolling a suburban after driving into a ditch
- Wrecking the side of a pickup truck while driving into a hole

I've had more successes than failures. However, it's certainly much easier to remember my driving mishaps than my routine nonevents. That's the problem with regret: it's a nagging reminder of what you could have done differently with no way to fix the past. I learned how *not* to wreck a snowmobile, how *not* to roll a suburban, and how *not* to drive into a hole. Einstein said that he never failed, he just found out what didn't work. Failure needs to be like that within our perspective. Failure released into the hands of the Holy Spirit diminishes the power of regret.

I've failed at things that I really wanted to succeed in. Failure to reach goals is disappointing. What I've learned is that God's purposes are better than my goals. If I allow the Holy Spirit to provide perspective in the middle of my failures, I gain understanding of what true success really is. Regret is self-pride delivering punishment that doesn't fit the crime. What more can you do about something that is in the past and cannot be redone? Letting go of the past failure will create perspective that will help shape your future. Perspective that is free from regret does not fear failure.

If you trust the deep work of the Holy Spirit, He will lead you to places that require His help for you to succeed. Where else can you risk it all while being completely confident that God has it all under control? His redeeming power is available to heal pain and loss. Knowing that provides assurance that everything we go through can be used for our good. The places that pose the biggest risk of loss are where the Holy Spirit works the greatest victory. Without the right perspective, through surrender, we'll never know the potential of what God can do in our lives.

The Benefit of Surrendered Perspective

20/20 vision is great. I wear contact lenses; it feels like I don't have a vision problem. Every night I clean the lenses before going to sleep. One night, I fell asleep before taking them out. I woke up the following morning and saw the details of the room. For a brief moment I thought, "I can see!" I then remembered I had forgotten to remove the contact lenses. Bummer.

A surrendered perspective means that I give God the benefit of the doubt in all situations. In times of testing that don't make sense, I trust God is working something within me that will build my character. I also know that His work in my life will further His plan for me. With a surrendered perspective, I'm not afraid to take risks that may lead to initial failure. Large projects that require a miracle don't intimidate me. I realize that the Holy Spirit provides the miracle to make something succeed. I also realize that participating in something bigger than myself will provide learning experiences for me to grow. For the fullness of the Holy Spirit to work within me, a dramatic display of my own weakness needs to be evident. This isn't prideful humility. It's an exercise in wisdom to know what the Holy Spirit is responsible for and what I am responsible for. The moment my weakness is present, God's strength is available.

Accurate perspective is a great benefit to a surrendered heart. We don't waste time in processing old situations. An accurate perspective gives you clear vision of the road in front of you. It might not provide the ability to see through mountains or around curves, but you can be assured that you'll see clearly with the right perspective.

CHAPTER THIRTEEN

CONTAGIOUS PEACE

Blizzards can be deadly or delightful depending upon your point of view and your location. Snow days are awesome for school-aged kids. Growing up in North Dakota, I spent many snow days listening to the wind roar outside our house and enjoying the warmth of a fire. On the other hand, people have died trying to walk through blizzards. In a blizzard, it's easy to become disoriented and die a few feet from safety. People have ventured from their homes or stranded cars in the midst of a blizzard, lost their way, and died mere yards from their front door. Without proper protection, nature's elements can cause severe damage.

Life is full of storms and stress. Possessing peace in the middle of a stressful life is a benefit of an aggressive surrender to the Holy Spirit. Peace provides the ability to be in the middle of chaos while being unmoved by the storm.

The Silent Killer

Stress damages physical and mental health. Stress causes people to gain weight, feel depressed, and lose hope. A documentary[5] illustrated the effect of stress on monkeys when a bully monkey wreaked havoc on the rest of the group. Those most affected by the bully did not have as much to eat. They became passive and gained weight from lack of sleep and constant secretion of adrenaline. When the bully monkey died from eating poison, everything stabilized for the other monkeys. Without providing an adequate answer, the narrator of the show asked viewers, "What can we learn from the monkeys that can help us decrease our stress level?"

I thought, *"What a stupid question. Apparently, the only thing we can learn is to kill the problem people in order to experience peace and tranquility."*

The documentary did a great job illustrating the dangers of stress and the problems that stress can cause. It didn't do a very good job of illustrating a peaceful solution. Problems do not easily go away. You cannot hit the reset button and restart the game when things go bad. You can, however, experience peace that goes beyond our understanding even in the middle of catastrophe. Look at these indicators that you may not be handling stress very well:

- Your mind constantly dwells on a problem you are facing.
- Your expectation level of yourself is too high. Failure is simply not an option.
- Your sleep is broken and minimal.
- You have a tough time letting go of things.

---

[5] National Geographic: Stress: Portrait of a Killer

- Your upcoming projects, requirements, or deadlines consume your thoughts.

Don't lose heart if you identified with any of these indicators. These are some of the most common indicators that almost everyone experiences. You are not alone.

The Solution

One of my favorite verses in the Bible is found in Isaiah 26:3 (ESV)

You will keep him in perfect peace whose mind is stayed on you, because he trusts in you.

Trusting the work of the Holy Spirit is the solution to our stress. He can be trusted. The only thing missing from the solution is our *choice* to focus our minds on God's ability. We have a choice. We can focus on things we cannot control or on the Holy Spirit who can work out everything.

One Sunday during church, I was tasked to give the announcements during the service. One announcement had a surprise. I advertised the upcoming dodge ball game for the young adults of our congregation. In the middle of that announcement, people began throwing balls at me while I was giving the details. I knew it was going to happen because I helped plan it, but it was still a challenge to remain focused on speaking while dodging. This should be an exercise for anyone who wants to become a public speaker.

Securing peace in your life can be as simple as remaining focused on God while flaming missiles are flying all around you. It is simple, but that doesn't make it easy. Focusing your vision on the solution in the midst of a meltdown brings a peace that will go beyond your natural understanding.

Let It Go

Ducks have an amazing ability to remain dry even after going underwater. On our farm, we had a few ducks and a pond for them to swim. Duck feathers have an oily substance that keeps them from becoming waterlogged. If you throw chickens in water, they will look like wet chickens. Throw ducks in the water, and they'll look dry even after diving and swimming for an hour.

Some people have gone through troubles and emerged like wet chickens. Other people have emerged from trials looking like a duck. The difference between the chicken and the duck is the ability to retain or roll water. Water from a pond rolls right off a duck's back. Let the water of your trial roll right off your back. No one looks like themselves when they are soaked.

Contagious Peace

It was a dry summer. The fire started while we were harvesting wheat. Someone first noticed the flames underneath the Chevy pickup. The fire started from dry straw accumulating and lodging next to the hot exhaust pipe. Since the pickup truck carried the fuel supply for the farm, it was a serious situation. Being the take-charge person that he was, Grandpa jumped into the pickup and drove it out of the field to save the crop. As Grandpa drove up the ditch that led to the gravel road, he lost traction and spun out. Meanwhile, the fire continued to burn underneath the frame. Family members shouted to Grandpa to get out of the pickup. Staying true to his stubborn German roots, he remained in the truck and eventually drove it onto the road where he accelerated to highway speed to put out the fire. I guess he thought the fire under the pickup was a like a candle to be blown out with the wind. It must have worked: there was no explosion.

During all this, up the road a couple of miles, my great-uncle Willie was preparing to unload a full truck of wheat. Over the CB radio he thought he heard, "Jason got run over by the pickup." In fact, my mom was talking on the CB and in mid-conversation told me to "get into the pickup!" In shock, he lost his sense of direction and backed down a ditch with a loaded truck and got stuck. Later that night, another friend who was helping us during the harvest listened to the story and nearly passed out from the drama. It was a night of chaos and was quite the opposite of peace.

Contagious peace is a benefit of an unconditional, aggressive surrender to the work of the Holy Spirit. People who are peacemakers have given God room to work in their lives. You can tell them by their qualities when under fire. Peacemakers are

- Calm under stress
- Able to think quickly
- Positive about the challenge they face
- Aggressive in their approach to bring resolution
- Conscious of other people's worry while seeking to calm their fears
- Able to realize God's hand at work in the situation no matter what the circumstances

The qualities of internal peace are displayed in the middle of war. The qualities of supernatural peace are strongest when the opposition is fierce. Can you bring peace to a situation that seems to be out of control? Can the strength of the Holy Spirit inside of you spill out to the weakness of the situation around you?

The peace you gain through focus on God in the middle of your trials will be the peace you give to others when you walk alongside them in their trials. Your peace is only as contagious as your trust in God during conflict. If you'd really like to make a difference in the lives of others, consider giving God a chance to make a big difference in the trials of your life. The peace that comes might surpass your ability to make sense of it. The peace that arrives will bring the perspective of God with it. Peace will be the strength that pulls you through the fire.

CHAPTER FOURTEEN

LINCOLN LOGS OR LUMBER?

The pressure of expectations weighed down the potential of pro quarterback Todd Marinovich. Todd's dad, Marvin, was a fitness coach and used Todd to explore the possibilities of raising a child in the perfect athletic environment. Weight training, nutritional discipline, and cardio exercise were steps of Todd's early childhood development. His future in the National Football League was being set up for failure through unrealistic expectations. Todd's struggle with drugs could be traced back to his inability to deal with overwhelming pressure in his life. All of the expectations of winning football games, dealing with a driven father, and the divorce of his parents prompted him to experiment with drugs and alcohol as a diversion from the chaos.

Pressure is common and not limited to celebrities or athletes. The amount of pressure differs from one person to another. Whatever the situation, surrendering to the Holy Spirit provides the outlet to withstand the pressures faced in a lifetime.

Aftermath of Devastation

In May 2011, an F-5 tornado blitzed through Joplin, Missouri. Homes disappeared, leaving only the foundation. More than 150 people died. For a community of 50,000, losing so many was felt by nearly every member of that community. In 2012, my wife and I were in Joplin. The weather was pretty nasty, and we stopped at a coffee shop. While we were there, the intense rain and wind prompted the tornado siren to go off. A hush fell over the coffee shop. A few people looked out the windows to see what might be coming their way. These people remembered what had happened not too long ago. Even in the middle of rebuilding their city, the pain of destruction was still a reality.

Having the Holy Spirit as the foundation of your life doesn't guarantee that you'll be untouched by life's storms, but it gives you the strength to rebuild as many times as you have been knocked down.

The Building Materials

Faith is our building material. If we build our faith on something that crumbles, we'll have wasted our faith and belief building upon the wrong thing. Faith is made up of several ingredients:

- **Confidence** provides the weight bearing function of a foundation.
- **Trust** is the supply of raw materials to give God something to work with.
- **Passion** is the supply of effort to partner with God in an endeavor.

Consider what happens when we place our faith on a poor foundation. If my faith is placed in my abilities, other people, or the uncertainty of wealth, there are several things that could happen:
- The moment I am unable to handle something, my confidence breaks. It's not easy to rebuild broken confidence.
- Each time that I fail, I will only strive harder to correct the failure and ensure that it never happens again. I will not trust God or people. In my pursuit of fixing things, I'll only cause more damage.
- When my goals aren't reached and my plan fails, my effort will be in low reserves. Why would I want to start over again and have to rebuild again?

These are problems when faith is built on the wrong thing. Ultimately, good resources are wasted.

We are angry when people in leadership fail because we wasted foundational building materials on them. It's not that people in leadership can't make a mistake; they (or we) always will. We are mad because we waste perfectly good portions of confidence, trust, and passion on something we think will make a difference but doesn't.

Built to Last

Faith built upon the foundation of the Holy Spirit can last through the storms. Building upon the Holy Spirit won't eliminate storms. The benefit of building upon the Holy Spirit is that the foundation remains.

In 1982, my dad and mom bought an old farmhouse for a dollar and moved it to its present-day location. Up north, we sometimes have trouble with basements flooding and becoming unusable. To counter that problem, they had a ground-up foundation built for the house. Instead of digging a hole, they had the foundation poured above ground and brought dirt to surround the walls of the foundation. That instantly created a slope for rain run-off and elevation for the lowest level of the house. Before the foundation was poured, the house was measured and fitted for a perfect match. A couple of years ago, my aunt and uncle built an addition on their house and a new foundation was needed. This one was a simple slab for the structure. During the pouring of the material, it didn't look like much. Once the walls went up, the building took shape based upon the plans and design of the foundation.

Working with the Holy Spirit is often like these two instances. In one case, the foundation may look different than what you've experienced before. The building process that you allow the Holy Spirit to do in your life might not be like what He's done before. Let Him do the work; He knows of situations that you know nothing about. In other cases, the foundation the Holy Spirit builds may not look like much initially. Wait until the walls of the structure begin going up. You'll see what He's doing and how much He's designed everything for your good.

The building materials of your faith (confidence, trust, and passion) help the Holy Spirit build things that last in your life. When we realize that our main function in building a project is to supply the materials, we free up the Holy Spirit to build as needed as long as we create the supply. It's exciting to realize that all I have to do is give God something to work with. He creates things that fit me, function well, and last.

A Last Word on Dealing With Pressure

Pressure, without the help and influence of the Holy Spirit, can tear anyone apart. It's like making a water bottle explode with dry ice. Take a 20 oz. plastic pop bottle, place water in it, add dry ice, screw on the top, and run like crazy. In a few seconds you'll have a boom like a firework without the smell of gunpowder. Pressures of life can be like the chunks of dry ice that create combustion. What remains unresolved in our hearts can create pressure. In contrast, a basketball or soccer ball is designed to take a beating yet retain its shape. It is built to withstand pressure and not be changed. The only time a ball will lose its shape is when it does something it is not designed to do (like get run over by a car).

Our lives can reflect either one of these objects: a bottle or a ball. The Holy Spirit helps us deal with the pressures of life to filter out the stress and retain our shape. The biggest difference between taking a beating or being blown up is our inclusion of the Holy Spirit's work in us. That shouldn't be a difficult choice.

CHAPTER FIFTEEN

IN MEMORY OF

If there was one thing in your life you wished for other people to remember you for, what would it be?

- **People are remembered for their leadership.** Presidents, business leaders, and military commanders fit this category. It's easy to document the actions evolving from their command.
- **People are remembered for their fame.** Singers, actors, and athletes who rise to prominence with their craft are often remembered during anniversaries of their death or significant moments relating to their industry.
- **People are remembered for their courage.** Revolutionaries and peaceful demonstrators who defied corrupt leaders and broken social systems are applauded for pioneering change.

What is a greater honor? Being remembered or being imitated? The Holy Spirit's work in our lives is to be remembered and is designed to inspire people to imitate Him. Leave a legacy of the Holy Spirit that can be passed on to the generation that follows. What will the Holy Spirit's legacy be in your life?

The Legacy of the Holy Spirit

Legacy is heritage. Heritage is something that was modeled to me through many generations. Heritage is usually reserved within the context of a family. The heritage and legacy of the Holy Spirit is meant to extend beyond the parameters of the earthly family. Consider the benefits of the Holy Spirit in these situations:

- **The Holy Spirit forms people through their surrender.** The drug addict who lived his life under the influence of substance abuse is healed and delivered from an addictive lifestyle. He decides to help other people form good habits and become free from addictions. His life is a beacon of credibility because of his personal victory. People are influenced by his life and remember and imitate him long after he's out of the picture.
- **The Holy Spirit empowers people.** Empowering someone means that you tap into the thing they were created to do. The woman who lacked confidence to pursue her dreams and desires is acquainted with the work of the Holy Spirit and realizes that she is now closer to fulfilling her dream. She trusts the work of the Holy Spirit and experiences confidence, hope, and vision. Because she understands empowerment, she is able to speak encouragement to other people and see the light bulb of hope begin to flicker in them. People who are influenced by her life will follow her example and trust the Holy Spirit in their own lives.
- **The Holy Spirit provides everything we need.** Contentment is eternal currency. Someone who has

walked with the Holy Spirit in tough times understands how to walk with someone else through a time of lack. This person is able to communicate simple terms of management and stewardship to someone else who is beginning their journey. People who are influenced by his life realize the value of stewarding what they have. They practice those principles long after their mentor is gone.
- **The Holy Spirit sustains us.** Endurance is built within people who withstand trouble. Since no one can control trouble, they realize their only hope is the sustaining work of the Holy Spirit. The young girl who is traumatized early in her life is sustained by the healing work of the Holy Spirit as she ages. Being sustained through trouble provides maturity and hope for a better future. She can relate to victims. She understands what they go through and how they feel. Because she trusted in the sustaining work of the Holy Spirit and clung to Him when things didn't make sense, she can articulate hope with clarity. People who are influenced by her life reciprocate her encouragement to someone else. Their overcoming perspective becomes contagious.
- **The Holy Spirit is love.** The love of God is poured into our hearts by the Holy Spirit. Accepting the work of the Holy Spirit in our lives means we accept the love of God. Accepting the love of God is a choice. He already loves us without measure; accepting the love provides a new level of liberty. The man who strove for significance with his work comes to understand that his effort doesn't cause God to love him more. He also realizes that his mistakes aren't excuses for God to love him less. When he consents to being loved by God with no conditions, his heart is free

from the insecurity that drove him to pursue significance. His significance is solid, and his understanding of God's love deepens. He helps other people realize God's love for them. As great as his work was, it still pales in comparison to the work of love through the Holy Spirit. Now a love for God fuels his mission and is contagious. People who are influenced by this man's love for God embrace God's love for their lives.

- **The Holy Spirit helps us become His legacy.** The fruit of His work that remains in us is love. Love is everything we need and it is what influences others. Love is the difference between simply being remembered and being imitated.

Imitate What Is Important

When we celebrated the life of my Grandpa George after his passing, four of his grandsons spoke at his funeral service. We planned a message that linked all of our talks to one central theme: *The only thing that matters is serving Jesus.* The theme was important to us because it was important to Grandpa. We didn't even talk about his accomplishments as a farmer, an upstanding community member, or a leader. We talked about the thing that mattered most—his spiritual life. Grandpa George was not remembered by the things he did. He is imitated because of what he became. It took him a while to surrender his life to Jesus, but when he did accept Christ's work on the cross for the forgiveness of his sins, he began a journey that made him who he was.

He leads. We follow.

When I love myself with most of my heart, following God is nearly impossible. Following is easy when we love God with our whole hearts. I can follow God and become perfected in love. I can trust Him and become something greater than I've ever been. I can experience greatness when I understand the power of submission. It's through my submission that I open the gateway for the Holy Spirit to enter. When He influences me with His leadership, I become changed.

My wrestling coach in college was an influence to me.[6] I followed his lead and became a better wrestler in two months. My improvement came upon the heels of my greatest disappointment. One of the things that helped me reach my potential was a conversation between my coach and a few of my teammates. In the middle of a meet-and-greet team event, Coach gathered a few of us freshmen and asked a few questions to get to know us better. He asked where we were from and our recent place winning at the state tournament. Many of the other freshmen had won a state wrestling tournament or placed highly. When it was my turn, all I could say was that I had placed my junior year but didn't win an award my senior year. Coach didn't even blink. He affirmed that the past really didn't matter because we were there to learn.

That's how we follow the lead of the Holy Spirit. The past doesn't matter when we're willing to surrender to His work towards the future. We're here to learn, and He's ready to help us grow. When we follow His lead, His influence in us influences others.

---

[6] He also thought it would be a great idea for us to go into the wilderness armed with nothing but a knife and live off the land. It would be a good character-building exercise.

He Empowers. We Experience.

Empowerment is the art of fueling the deepest desire of the heart. Empowerment from the Holy Spirit is the art of revealing the desires of the heart that were built in by the Creator. We experience fulfillment through empowerment. We may not realize what we have inside of us. Empowerment is experienced through obedience. When I love God more than I love myself, I stop trying to figure out who I am and discover who God says I am. People are imitated when they live how they were meant to live. They have the most influence when they are brave enough to do what God wants them to do.

If you want to be imitated after you're gone, you'll need to make your life a legacy. Love makes the important things matter. Love helps retain focus on priority. Love helps us act like the Holy Spirit. Love is what makes our temporary lives influential. When you love God more than you love yourself, you'll discover exactly what you were created for. You'll understand the people you were meant to reach. You'll find the greatest fulfillment by being who you were meant to be. Loving God is how you leave a legacy. That's the best benefit of surrender to the Holy Spirit.

CHAPTER SIXTEEN

ARE YOU GOOD ENOUGH?

It is frustrating to work on a project and have it dismissed by someone else. Frustration builds when expectations are not communicated before beginning a job. Do you ever feel as if your whole life is based upon a series of unaccepted works? This is how many people live. They believe that if they work hard enough, they can gain God's favor and His love. While they mean well, their works are an obstacle to their surrender. I heard a public speaker talk about his religious upbringing. The church his family attended had strict rules concerning conduct and dress. He lived under pressure to meet those expectations. Unfortunately, his attempts never fulfilled the expectations. The bar was simply raised higher and higher. I remember his statement: "What I did was never good enough."

Trying to earn significance can complicate unconditional surrender. Significance cannot be earned. Significance has to be accepted.

God's Way

For years, I prayed for a relative of mine to accept Christ. Uncle Willie always went to church, was generous with his money, and had a kind heart towards people. For the majority of his life, he lived in the tension of being a good person while knowing that he wasn't completely surrendered to God. Early in his life, he and his brothers were in church one Sunday when the pianist had a heart attack and died at the piano. They were the first ones out the door.

One morning, Uncle Willie was rushed to the hospital. His heart had stopped, and it looked like he was not going to make it. The ambulance rushed him to a hospital seventy miles away. The doctors had little hope that he would wake up. Even if he did wake up, they said he'd most likely be brain-dead. Many people prayed for him. Uncle Willie did wake up and was coherent. When he awoke, my aunt Jenny was in the room and began talking with him. When she told him that his heart had stopped, the reality of life without Christ impacted him. He made his decision that day to accept the significance of Christ's work for him. One of the things he said after his prayer was that he never felt good enough to accept Jesus. He was always trying to be a good person that was worthy of God's love.

That perspective is what keeps millions of people at arm's length from God's love. Our own pride tells us we must be worthy of unconditional love and that we must work to deserve it. The deepest desire of our heart is to be accepted, while the deepest desire of our pride is to take the credit. According to pride, what good is something if it cannot be earned? What good is a benefit if it cannot be repaid? To embrace unconditional surrender to God, we have to be willing to offer unfinished projects, imperfect character, and ulterior motives. God wants to influence us now, in all of our imperfections.

Only God could accept the imperfections of our work and trade them with the perfection of a finished work of forgiveness. That finished work is God's offering to each one of us. The work of Christ on the cross and the life of the Spirit are available. He did it all. Our role is to accept that work and allow His work inside of us. That's God's way.

The Biggest Obstacle of All

A loveless life is like a cancer to the soul. This feeling drives people to damaging conclusions. It causes people to take their lives, take advantage of others, and think only of themselves. Trying to earn love that already exists creates insanity. When dealing with impending failure, do you go to extremes to correct it? When facing loss, do you blame yourself for something that you had no control over? Are you concerned about how you appear to other people? Under stressful circumstances, does your mind constantly race for solutions at the cost of your personal relationships? If you answered yes to any of these questions, you may need to rethink your perspective concerning how God sees you. Consider these ideas:
- You can view your failures as learning experiences. You can't change the past, but you can learn from it.
- Take a step back during loss and see if you can find the hand of God at work. It may be that He is doing something deeper than you give Him credit for.
- Find out who you really are based on the abilities, gifts, and unique perspective that God has given you. Don't base your conduct or answers to questions on what you think people want to hear from you. Base

your actions and thoughts on who God has created you to be.
- Learn how to trust God with things you cannot control. Talk with God and ask Him to do things on your behalf that you cannot do on your own.

These statements might help you identify the obstacles in your journey of surrender. You may find that the biggest obstacle of all is in the mirror.

Listen Closely and Follow Correctly

The second sin recorded in the Bible was a man murdering his brother. The murder followed the rejection of an offering. God had accepted the offering of a lamb over the offering of vegetables. Both men wanted to offer their best, but God accepted only one. Cain's offering of vegetables was based upon the work of his own hands. Abel's lamb offering was based upon faith.[7] Cain had an opportunity to learn from his effort but would not accept God's constructive criticism. In his view, God had not accepted him. In God's view, He had not accepted Cain's offering. Cain misunderstood what God was trying to say to him and became angry with God, killing Abel in the process.

I was an independent and very stubborn child. At a young age, I thought I could dress myself and made it known to my mother that I could do it myself. You know what happens when a little child dresses himself? It doesn't look very good. Eventually, I learned that it is good to have help. For some of us, that takes a long time. For others, receiving help is not a big deal.

---

[7] Hebrews 11:4

God Provides

If you struggle with unconditional surrender to the Holy Spirit, you might be trying to present an offering to appease a god that you've misunderstood. You can't earn God's love. The love that He has reserved with our names on it is limitless and cannot be earned with anything we say or do. It also cannot be diminished by anything we say or do. The love that God provides is completely and unconditionally available. This love is based on the significance that we've been created with. God has already placed worth, meaning, and importance upon each one of us. If you can accept God's love for you just as you are you'll be on your way to overcoming the obstacle of trying to present an offering of your own work. He just wants you.

Consider the places in your life where you are striving for something. Inspect the areas where stress is causing harm. Think about the work that God desires to do in you and with you. He is able to redeem, restore, and rebuild whatever is broken. Instead of trying to place an offering of your work on the altar, consider removing the offering built by your hands and placing yourself on that altar for God to work through. Your life as an offering will have significant influence on others as God demonstrates His love in you and through you.

CHAPTER SEVENTEEN

THE UNBELIEVER'S IDENTITY

Costumes can trick people. My grandma Avis looks like the granny in the Tweety Bird cartoons. She wore her hair up in a bun for a long time. Before I was born, my grandma and grandpa went to a costume party with many of their friends. Grandma literally let down her hair, dressed up like a witch, and fooled the entire crowd. No one knew it was her.

On another occasion, a group of students was traveling to northern North Dakota to work with a church. The students were going to stay in homes of the congregation, and my parents volunteered to open their small home to a few of the students. They were scheduled to meet at the corner of Highway 81 and Highway 5 to pick up the kids and bring them back to their house. It just happened to be Halloween that night, and my folks had some costumed guests that stopped by. Just before the students were picked up, someone thought it would be hilarious to have Steve and Gordy pick up the kids. Steve was dressed as a Neanderthal woman, and Gordy was dressed as Superman. They were to pose as Bob and LeAnn, the homeowners. The scheduled pickup time was late in the evening, providing complete darkness. Gordy and Steve drove to the meeting place where the van full of students was waiting. As they walked towards the van, illuminated by the lights, there was complete silence inside the van until one of the students said, "Man! That is one ugly woman! Let's get out of here!"

Grandma's friends couldn't recognize her, and the college students couldn't identify Steve. Those around us have a hard time seeing our true identity when we base our identity upon the limitation of our own perspective.

Identity Revealed

Whenever we depend upon our experience to confirm our identity, we will have a hard time understanding the identity that God created within us. Because identity can be blurred with little lies, it's easy for us to become confused with who we really are. The Holy Spirit can help us confirm our identity when we trust Him completely.

BELIEF IN "ME"	BELIEF IN GOD
I determine the direction of my life.	I've decided to follow Jesus.
I don't care much about people.	I believe in kindness and being tenderhearted towards others.
I can be insecure.	I am confident because of God's love for me.
I use people to improve my position.	My position in life is a platform for serving others.
I'm a pretty good person.	Jesus has paid for my sin. I'm righteous because of him.
My identity is based on what I do.	My identity is based on who God says I am.
I attempt things if I'm sure I will succeed.	With God, nothing is impossible.

The Obstacle of Me

I limit the work and power of the Holy Spirit in my life when I do things on my own and depend upon my own ability and resources. This problem has been here from the beginning. If I don't have to depend upon God, I'll take credit for coming up with solutions on my own. My identity can be skewed without the influence of the Holy Spirit.

The slightest degree off-course can change the destination. I was not a great math student in high school but I did learn a few things. In geometry, I learned that one degree could make a big difference. If a line is one degree off, it affects the destination point. Without the guidance of the Holy Spirit, it's easy for our identity to become skewed and to miss the point.

I was sixteen when I felt a call to focus on the inner cities of America. In most cases, people who are from a city understand the dynamics of cities. People who grow up on farms understand the context of a farm. Here I was, sensing a call to go to a place I had never experienced or known. I pursued that call through education and experience. My degree in Urban Ministries tells the world that I've studied and passed the tests to be certified. My experience in working with churches and other community groups displays a competence in what I do.

My journey hasn't been easy. I had doubts, and feared that my lack of credibility would diminish my personal influence. I feared that I would encounter some circumstance bigger than me and mingle with people who wouldn't accept me. I was striving for the identity of an urban practitioner. The day that my identity began to change from *what* I did to *who* I trusted happened beside a construction truck a few miles south of Canada. Up to this time, I was trying to figure out my purpose and identity by what I did. An urban practitioner is not an urban practitioner when working road construction in rural North Dakota. It seemed I was very far away from this calling.

I stood next to the truck and in my heart told God that if He wanted me to work road construction for the rest of my life, I would do it if that's what brought Him joy. It was then that I realized the joy that God feels has never been based on what I can do for Him; God's joy is based upon how much I trust Him. He doesn't need my help to change the inner cities of the world. He wants my help because if He does work through me, He receives the glory. How could a farm boy make a difference in a city unless it was the Holy Spirit working through him?

The day that I changed my identity from being me-based was the day I began a journey of discovering who I am created to be through trusting the work of the Holy Spirit. I'm still learning who I am, but I am confident with my identity being revealed. I don't worry so much about how I feel or what I struggle with; I turn that energy to trusting God with who He is making me to be.

Remove the obstacle of self-belief and believe in the Holy Spirit's process. Believing in the self is the counterfeit to trusting the work of the Holy Spirit and understanding the identity that He's creating in you. Trusting the work of the Holy Spirit carries the real value.

CHAPTER EIGHTEEN

LUNATICS FOR SURVIVAL

I've been hearing more stories about sinkholes. In August 2013, a Florida sinkhole opened up near Disney World and destroyed an apartment complex. *National Geographic*'s online article[8], "Why Sinkholes Open Up", presents this description of a sinkhole:

> *A sinkhole is basically any collapsed or bowl-shaped feature that's formed when a void under the ground creates a depression into which everything around it drains. The cover-collapse sinkhole is the one that makes the news. It tends to occur in clay, because clay holds soil together like glue. Soil leaches into a cave below and creates a void in the soil that moves upward. You can't see it on the surface. Then, all of the sudden, the bridge over top of that void can't hold anymore and it collapses.*

---

[8] http://news.nationalgeographic.com/news/2013/08/130812-florida-sinkhole-disney-world-explainer-urban-science/

Some people behave just like sinkholes by draining those around them. These people can be described as high-maintenance, vampires, drama magnets, and whirlwinds of destruction. It's easy to label someone with the same affliction we all try to hide. All of us have sinkholes in our hearts that drain our spiritual resources. These sinkholes are the unresolved issues that keep us from fully surrendering to the life that the Holy Spirit provides for us.

These issues could be

- **Wounds that haven't healed.** Someone hurt your heart and you haven't been able to remove yourself from their influence by forgiving them.
- **An inner thirst that isn't quenched.** The approval you've strained for all of your life never came from the person you wanted to please.
- **The hunger that isn't fulfilled.** Significance is fleeting. You've tried to build your worth through great accomplishments, but there always seems to be something missing.
- **Sleep that flees with no rest in sight.** Storm after storm pummels your life. There seems to be nothing you can do about difficult situations. They are constant, steady, and relentless. You can't catch your breath.

All of these issues keep us from unconditional surrender. It's not that we don't want to surrender; we simply know no other way to live but in survival mode. The mode of survival is the deepest type of self-centeredness. The danger in this type of living is that we don't even realize how inward focused we've become.

Healed the First Time

Never try to go down a half-pipe ramp with a skateboard unless you've skated before. Of course, I learned the hard way. I broke my leg and ankle riding a skateboard down a ramp. Consequently, I received a medical screw in my ankle to guide the healing process. Four months after the accident, the doctors removed the screw and my ankle returned to normal.

During high school, my cousin Dale broke his arm and had to wear a cast. During a check-up with the doctor, they realized the bone was not healing correctly. The doctor took Dale's arm in his hands, slowly inspected the break, and suddenly, without warning, re-broke the arm. In the moment, it was horrifying. Years later, it's now hilarious. Special attention was needed for the broken bones in both circumstances. In both cases, the healing process demanded drastic actions. The broken bones would not heal on their own and needed guides to help heal correctly.

Broken people need guides during healing. We need to be healed the first time we go through the process. The process lengthens when we fail to learn healing after being broken. Have you wondered why you go through things again and again? Sometimes a problem can repeat itself, and it feels like an endless cycle of experiencing the same thing in different expressions. In *Groundhog Day*, the main character wakes up to the same day over and over again. I would hate to wake up to the same monotony day after day. When we fail to embrace healing from trauma, we place ourselves in the position of waking up to the same thing every single morning.

If we cannot embrace healing, we become lunatics for our own survival. We are the only thing we think about, care about, and act upon. It can seem right at the time. That's what makes it so dangerous. We don't even realize that our own actions of survival are keeping us from the benefit of surrender.

Rich's Story

Rich and his wife were both diagnosed with stage four cancer. Instead of accepting the diagnosis and preparing to die, they embraced the possibility of their healing and made plans to live. By living, they traveled to different churches and shared their story. They continued to serve and love people and wrote "*Through the Valley*", the story of their journey.[9]

Rich worked with me during one of my community outreach events in Moorhead, MN. He was in charge of the tent where our guests could pray with someone. Two nights prior to the event, we were at the site preparing for a leaders' meeting in the prayer tent. Standing there before the meeting, he was overcome with emotion because he had the privilege of helping other people pray with our guests. It was one of those moments of heartfelt appreciation for being able to help someone else. Rich's perspective defined his healing. He was completely surrendered to the process that God was asking him to walk through. Even during the loss of his wife in late 2013, his posts on Facebook continued to reflect his willingness to work with God in the current process of his life.

He struggled at times with his hope. During another one of our community events, he mentioned to me that he was struggling with discouragement. He was human. Every one of us would struggle with the trial that he walked though. The thing that set Rich apart from other people was his focus on

---

[9] http://www.amazon.com/Through-Valley-Richard-Johnson/dp/1449797962

fixing his heart on hope. That's what enabled him to speak, write, and communicate the possibility of God's intervention in the middle of his trouble. Rich joined his wife, Robin, in Heaven early in 2014. While their time on earth may have been shorter than normal, their impact on earth has remained.

Healing is not always measured by how the body feels or how the mind responds. Healing begins with the fixation on hope and is completed with the fullness of surrender. People who haven't surrendered their hearts completely to the Holy Spirit's work will measure His work by their own standards and will ponder questions like these:

- Why haven't you answered my prayer?
- Why didn't you heal the ones I love before they died?
- Why is there no relief in sight?

These measuring standards create selfishness. We don't mean to be selfish. Nobody wants to be that person. I've never met someone who said, "When I was born, selfishness was my goal!" They became self-centered because they didn't fill the sinkholes of their heart with the healing perspective of the Holy Spirit. Their own standards of measurement actually created larger sinkholes that became dangerous to everyone around them.

When You've Done Everything, Just Stand

After you've done everything you know to do concerning your situation, you simply need to let it rest. However, if you simply have to do something, I'd suggest you look to serve someone else. One of the greatest ways to fill a sinkhole in your heart is to help someone else. Instead of trying to find material to fill the void, let the Holy Spirit work on that while you work on something else right in front of you.

Make sure you serve people for their benefit, not for your own. Don't just pick a person and make them a project.

In Memphis, TN, a teenager's heart was changed through serving someone else. A dad and his son served at a Convoy of Hope event. Since it was a Saturday morning, the teenage son was not thrilled to be up so early and spend the entire day in the summer heat. The boy let his dad know exactly how he felt through his silence and sulking. One of the guests came to the outreach event in a wheelchair. She lived a couple of blocks from the site and pushed herself in the wheelchair all the way to the event. It just so happened that the teenager's path intersected with our disabled guest as she received her groceries. As she prepared to leave, our guest needed help getting back to her home. The teenager was moved in his heart with compassion and asked his dad if he could help her home. The dad said yes.

On their way home, the teenager was quiet again. This time, it wasn't the quiet of sulking or being angry, it was the quiet of contemplation. His dad asked him what he was thinking and how he was feeling, and the boy shared his experience. Upon arriving at the guest's home, he had realized there was no ramp accessibility for a wheelchair to enter the house. Something could be done about that. He wondered if they could go back to her house and build her a ramp. A ramp would help her get into her house much easier. A couple of weeks later, father and son built a ramp into the house. A bridge of compassion was also built into a teenager's heart through a simple act of service.

Serving other people is most effective when we don't feel like doing it. This young lad is the perfect example of what happens in the heart of the server when they become available for the Holy Spirit to work through. If we respond in obedience to the request right in front of us, the sinkholes in our hearts will be filled by the Holy Spirit. Getting what we need becomes secondary to giving something away.

CHAPTER NINETEEN

I'LL DO IT BETTER

The summer after high school graduation, I worked on a ranch in western North Dakota. Part of my job was to feed cattle with pellets hauled in a pickup truck. During one of the feed runs, my coworker and I traveled up a small hill with a large hole on the left side of the road. We made a mental note to avoid that hole on the way back. On our way back, we remembered the hole, but I thought it was on my left side of the road. Apparently, I was thinking in mirror images that day. I moved the pickup truck to the right, crested the hill, and drove straight into the hole I had been trying to avoid. A mirror image doesn't always demonstrate the correct perspective. A pitfall to our influence is when we think we are doing the right thing but, like a mirror image, is actually backwards.

Nothing Changed

During one football season, our intramural team was losing every game. A couple of us decided that if we lost another game, we were going to take over certain positions on the team that others held. We were upperclassmen and thought that we could do whatever we wanted. We lost the next game, took over, and continued to lose. That went well. Thinking that we could do it better, we simply helped prolong a level of mediocrity when we worked as individuals instead of working as a team. Individuals who sabotage the direction of a team for their personal ambition never help the situation.

In the process of surrendering to the complete work of the Holy Spirit, there will be times when you work with people who might not do something as well as you. You'll need to learn how to let the Holy Spirit work out the details before you charge in to fix things. Strong personalities have trouble with this. It's obvious to them what the solution is, and if nobody is willing to do anything about it, they will. Sometimes these situations are a test of your surrender to the Holy Spirit's leading. The Holy Spirit works through different people to accomplish God's purposes on earth. Can you imagine the complexity of coaching this diverse group of people who are on same team? In our haste to do things right or better, our actions could sabotage the Holy Spirit's coaching in others.

The next time that you feel you could do something better than the person beside you or ahead of you, consider the fact that God might be leading the other person through a growing process. In your effort to do it right, you might be interfering with the Holy Spirit's work in their lives.

Don't Do That Again

There are times that we only learn through a bad experience. An electric fence is a great deterrent to wandering. On our farm, we fenced pigs and cows using a simple little wire that emitted a small electrical shock when touched. After just a few encounters, the animals were convinced to stay in the fence. We would be wise to know the boundaries of our

surrender so God can be free to work out the details. Here are some indicators that you might be pushing the boundaries of your surrender:
- You constantly criticize the decisions of your superiors.
- You tell people how you would do something differently.
- You only tell the people above you what they want to hear because you care more about your success than the success of others.
- You gather a posse of people to support you.
- You exaggerate your greatness and importance.

There's a good chance that everyone has done one of these things at some time. The point is to determine whether or not these are consistent indicators of your attitude towards others. Your attempt to fix things or gain leadership may be the very thing keeping you from becoming fully prepared for the plans God has for you. Before acting, think about your motives.

The Mirror Image

Like my little accident with the pickup truck, it can seem that you're doing the right thing, only to be mistaken and plunge into a hole. Taking charge of a situation can seem right, and in some cases it might be right. Being able to contribute to the processes of God is not based on our ability to lead, administrate, or find a solution. Being able to contribute is based on listening and discerning a situation. If you've ever been mistaken in your zeal to make something right, take heart. You can always try again and learn how to do it differently. Can you tell the difference between reality and the mirror image? Consider these indicators:

- Time. God works on a timetable that is not ours. Our timetable might be our lifetime; God's timetable may extend beyond our lifetime. Wait-and-see is a proactive approach to a situation without clear direction. Wait on God, and see what He's doing. God is at work in the heart of another, and if we trust His work, we'll give Him the time to do what He needs to.
- Peace. If you are uneasy about a situation, you need to consider the peace (or lack of it) inside of you. There are times you'll need to act when you're afraid. It's one thing to act when you're nervous, and another thing when you know it's the wrong decision. I joined a direct sales company at great expense when deep down, I knew it wasn't the right decision. I was swayed by the possibility of making money and completely ignored the lack of peace within me. I thought that by taking this "leap of faith" into this company, I'd make money and show my ability to be fearless in a new venture. It didn't end well because I acted without peace.
- Wisdom. There are some situations that can be discerned by using common sense, but sometimes the answer must come from godly wisdom.
- Obedience. We can listen to instruction or learn things the hard way. Sometimes God tells us things we don't like or want to hear. God is gracious enough to give us a choice and is holy enough to ensure that we learn what we need to. Following instructions should simply be done, not talked about.

Learn to Discern

We can know God's heart through the Holy Spirit. If I give the Holy Spirit access to my heart, I'll truly know my motives. It's an art to learn how to respond to the words of the Holy Spirit. If we listen to the words the Holy Spirit speaks to us, we'll discern the difference between when the Holy Spirit is speaking to our hearts and when our hearts may be leading us astray.

A few years ago, I was in an irritating place. I was underpaid and looking for new opportunities. My frustration grew, as doors of opportunity remained closed. I thought for sure that I was in transition and on the way out. I was right, but I didn't have the right timing. When my wife and I made the decision to endure and wait for God to work things out, peace settled in and grace gave us strength. There were some tough times during the following months, but the earlier angst of frustration was no longer there. It had been replaced with an ability to wait on God's work.

Five months after our decision to endure, the door opened for a new opportunity. A fresh new season was upon us, and we could enjoy a new era. If I had continued to push and prod in my frustration, the door may not have opened to the new season. By giving God the room to work in our situation and in our lives, He prepared us for what He had planned for us.

Remember this: if you're at the point of no return and are tempted to take matters into your own hands, God can still do it better than any one of us. Even on our best day, God's work is more reaching and effective. Let Him do what He needs to do. He'll let you know what you need to do. Best of all, He'll prepare you for the plans He has for you.

CHAPTER TWENTY

I'M IN MY OWN WAY

College tests didn't worry me. I wasn't consistent in preparing for them. I earned passing grades on my tests during the first part of each semester, but I had problems on the next test. I had the same amount of time to study for the next test, but I thought I'd pass based on my history of doing well on the previous test. I attended class but didn't study for the next test because I was riding the success of the previous test.

One of the hardest times to continue a growth-based aggressive surrender is during seasons of success. Poverty may hurt you but sudden success might kill you. When things are good, it's tough to trust God like we do when things are bad. Our hearts are inclined to take it easy. The path of least resistance seems to offer the best deals. When things are good, it's easy to lean on past success in hopes that it will carry you through.

Super Bowl-winning teams face this problem after their victories. It's harder to stay on top than to climb to the top. Part of the struggle may be that the journey has ended for the winners. They have met their goal, and there is no further destination except to win again. The team that wins the big game sometimes has credit mongers demanding a bigger payday. There's nothing wrong with being given the value that you bring to an organization. What makes things wrong is the credit that individuals claim for the team's win, emphasizing themselves over their teammates. If hindsight is 20/20 vision, success might be the beginning of an eye disease.

New Levels

Success can be good. In fact, when used correctly, you can actually grow in levels of surrender when you realize the credit belongs to the Holy Spirit. All measures of success are awards that fade when compared to the level of growth still available for a surrendered individual. A professor of mine once said, "The longer the shoreline of knowledge, the greater the continent of ignorance." The more you know, the more you need to learn. The greater you become, the more you need to serve. The higher your level of influence, the more you need to depend upon God to build the internal infrastructure of character to withstand the weight of that influence.

A new level might look completely different than what you're used to. Sarah Edgar was a phenomenal ice skater. In her elementary school years, she trained in Canada and later in Minneapolis. Her dedication helped her climb to new levels of excellence and into the possibilities of international and Olympic competition. The sacrifice that each new level demanded competed with the health of her family. Training for new levels of success was a strain. Training in a city six hours from your house makes family relationships hard to maintain. The Edgars made the choice to discontinue ice skating for the good of their family.

Some people might view this as a waste of potential. What Sarah gave up for temporary rewards, she focused on causes that mattered in eternity. Using her platform as Ms.

Teen North Dakota, she helped bring awareness to hungry children in Haiti. She is a role model of character and consistency. God has great plans for this young lady. All of this might not have happened if she had continued striving for awards and success measured by ribbons and medals. Because she was willing to start over and rebuild something, she is someone that God uses to champion His causes.

Growing in the Middle of Success

If you want to grow when you have it all, you have to be willing to rebuild, relinquish, and restore. Success is like the wind: some days it's all around you, and other days you can't find a wisp of it. Success is fleeting and is not guaranteed. Being willing to rebuild is more of a mindset than an action. Every single day, we rebuild by getting up in the morning, getting ready, and being ready for whatever faces us. Effort and ability are available to start over; it's the mind that presents the argument. It's hard to let go of something you've worked hard for and are proud of.

Orville and Yvonne Carlson had to start over after their missionary assignment in East Pakistan. It was their first mission. They boarded the ship with their children and possessions to travel across the sea. Once in India, Orville built a church. Their children—Randy, Rita, and Renee—grew up and learned the language. After living in the tropics for many years, Yvonne became sick and had to come back to the United States. Her doctor advised them not to return to East Pakistan. The climate would damage her health. They needed to look at a new mission in a new place.

A new mission opened up in Fiji, an island in the middle of the Pacific. Orville and Yvonne were willing to start over even after their investment in East Pakistan. They didn't know what was ahead of them, but they trusted God and were willing to begin again. They let go of their success in East Pakistan for the possibility of something great in Fiji. Once in Fiji, Orville built a Bible college. Orville was the chief architect and contractor of the school. He leveled a mountain with a Caterpillar to build the school. Since he held every position in the construction of the school, all he had to do was change hats in the morning. Orville and Yvonne had many years of successful ministry in Fiji before they retired. Since their earthly retirement, both Orville and Yvonne have retired from life on earth and gone to their heavenly reward.

The college that Orville built is still going strong. In 2012, my dad and mom had the opportunity to train students at the Bible college in Fiji. They taught students to build water filters and explained gardening techniques and cooking tools that could be used in remote village locations. Orville and Yvonne Carlson helped make the training in 2012 a reality through their willingness to rebuild and start over. One mission produced a church; the second mission produced a school. Being willing to rebuild can have an impact on multiple generations.

Credit Makes Enemies. Let's Stay Friends.

When you experience success, you have to be willing to share credit. None of your success is the result of your work alone. All of your success has another person's help in the process. This lesson was played out with soap opera-style drama in the Dallas Cowboys football team. Their owner, Jerry Jones, purchased the team in 1988. He promptly fired the legendary coach Tom Landry and brought in a college coach named Jimmy Johnson. Jimmy and Jerry were friends and teammates during their college years at the University of Arkansas.

Jimmy and Jerry defined their roles. Jimmy coached; Jerry owned. It worked out well until they started winning. Winning a Super Bowl brought out the credit hog in both of them. Jerry wanted more credit as the owner and general manager; Jimmy wanted credit as coach and wanted Jerry to stick to his role as an owner. After their second Super Bowl win, Jerry and Jimmy called it quits. Jimmy resigned and Jerry brought in another coach. Bad blood remained between them. Jerry said that any coach could have won the Super Bowl with that team. Maybe he was right. But we'll never know how many Super Bowls the team could have won if both men shared the credit.

People who want to sustain their success and grow in surrender to the Holy Spirit have to be willing to relinquish the credit and possibly receive no recognition from anyone on earth. Those who are able to let go of the credit realize the only scorecard that matters is being tallied in heaven.

Don't Be Afraid of the Dirt

If you're going to manage success well, you'll also have to be willing to restore. The cast of the TV show *Overhaulin'* restores old, junky cars. Most people overlook old vehicles because it takes a lot of effort and money to restore them to how they were intended to be. People who restore get their hands dirty helping someone else become who God intended them to be. Surrendered people don't count how much it will cost them to help restore someone; they recognize overlooked value in someone else and make the effort to help.

Someone who is willing to help restore another person will always be a candidate for great success. The only way you can continue to climb to greater heights without getting a bigger head is to remember how God restored you. You had nothing to do with the work that God performed. The only thing that contributed to God's work in you was your availability to be worked on. It was your surrender that paved the way for transformation. It's your willingness to help someone else experience their transformation that will keep you from succumbing to success and becoming useless in God's kingdom. Don't get in your own way of surrender by thinking your success had something to do with you. There's no limit to what God can do through you if you handle success well.

CHAPTER TWENTY-ONE

SPINACH OR KRYPTONITE?

During high school, our football team hosted a Lift-a-Thon to raise money for the athletic department. The object was simple. Football players raised funds by asking their friends and family to pledge financial amounts in proportion to weight lifted on the bench press. I approached Uncle Willie and asked him if he would pledge money for our upcoming contest. At first he thought about pledging a dollar per pound until he realized that I would probably lift over 200 pounds in this competition. He quickly adjusted the amount.

One of the obstacles of a complete surrender is the benefit of our own strength. To become the person that God has created you to be, you need to realize that your greatest strength can become your greatest obstacle. Why would that be a problem in an unconditional surrender to the Holy Spirit? The journey of your spiritual life with the Holy Spirit is not dependent upon how strong you are; your journey is dependent upon your ability to follow the Holy Spirit in the middle of your weaknesses.

Finding Strength

I rarely enjoy tests but I took a test that changed that. My cousin Dale gave my wife Natalie and I the book *StrengthsFinder 2.0*. The *StrengthsFinder* test is a test by Dr. Donald O. Clifton and Gallup that identifies your top five strengths out of a list of 34 unique qualities. Dale told us to take the test before reading the strengths listed in the book. He didn't want the strengths we read about to influence the way we took the test. We followed his advice and took the test. The results were so accurate they were almost eerie. Natalie and I identified with the test results and how best to use them. A couple of years later, I retook the test and two of my strengths had shifted based on the work that I was doing at the time. Three of the core strengths remained the same. Both tests were still very accurate.

A benefit of working with a team of people is that their strengths can complement your weaknesses. Any good team will celebrate individuals' strengths while using them to cover others' weaknesses. In fact, only poor leaders revel in their team's weaknesses. It's one of the ways they cover their own insecurities. Because of those behaviors, most of us have been trained to focus on building our individual strengths while covering our weaknesses. Building strength is a good thing. Finding strength in the Lord when He works through your weaknesses is the best thing. How do you do that?

Just Show Up

The Holy Spirit works through people who show up. While God can work through our weaknesses, He won't work through our invisibility. I'm convinced many miracles go undone because people fail to show for their calling. I had the privilege of touring a neighborhood in Staten Island, NY. It was a place most people avoid. The housing projects are reminders of poverty in the neighborhood. In the middle of that neighborhood was a bright spot called New Hope Community Church. There are programs for kids and adults, and a love for the community is evident. The pastor, David Beidel, and his family have been in the community for over twenty years. What Pastor Dave is doing in Staten Island demonstrates the audacity to respond to the call of God. As we drove through the neighborhood, my heart was slightly overwhelmed.

The Holy Spirit works well when we show up for an assignment. Even if we don't have all the goods and tools necessary to complete a task, we can still show up so that God is given the opportunity to work redemption. He needs us to show up and be present. He's proven over and over again that He'll do the rest.

Not Alone

Derek Sivers gave a TED talk on how to start a movement. To start a movement, you need to get people to dance. For starters, you need a crazy individual. Preferably someone brave. He must be willing to look completely foolish dancing by himself until he convinces another person to dance with him. The second person is very important to the life of the dance. It shows the world that there is one person who believes in dancing just as much as the crazy guy. If possible, it's good if they can bring along two or three people. At some point, while the music is playing and the group dances, others will join in and the critical mass swings in favor of the dancers vs. the spectators. It's only a matter of time until the whole crowd joins the fun of looking foolish. Tracking the critical mass is hard to do because it just happens.

Becoming a leader of movements isn't about the strength of an individual. It's about the willingness of that individual to follow the initiative of the Holy Spirit. The Holy Spirit brings people to a place they've never been before. In order to arrive at a new destination, we should be willing to take steps on an unknown journey. You can always tell the people who understand what walking with the Holy Spirit means by their attitudes:

- They are confident in their journey of life.
- They don't need the approval of others to make a decision.
- They are willing to go into dark areas of the world to be a light of God's presence.
- They never make someone else feel lesser because of their own revelation.
- They are not just followers, but leaders-in-training.
- They are intentional in bringing others along on the journey.

The foundation of their thinking is built upon the reality that they are not alone. Confidence built from knowing who leads them drives them to great purposes. They understand what it means to lean on the strength of the Holy Spirit.

How to Walk

Glacier National Park is a hiker's paradise. To see the majesty of nature, it's best to travel on hiking trails apart from the main roads. Many years ago, my dad, my brother, and I hiked over twenty miles in the span of three days. In our preparation, we made sure we had enough water, food, and supplies; we wore proper attire for the environment; we packed the map; and we were set. Walking with the Holy Spirit is not rocket science. There are many similarities to a regular walk, in fact.

- Water. Water consumption is vital on a hike. Without water, you will dehydrate quickly. Walking with the Holy Spirit requires constant consumption of the Holy Spirit's encouragement and the love of God. These sources of refreshment will sustain you on your journey.
- Food. When you embark on a long hike, you must pack food to fuel you on your journey. The fuel for your spiritual journey is knowledge about the Holy Spirit, and you must be intentional about seeking it out. Learning, and applying, new things about the character of God will strengthen your next steps.
- Proper attire. When you hike, you must wear the correct shoes and clothing to handle any anticipated problems. For example, you wouldn't wear a t-shirt in a blizzard. On your walk with the Holy Spirit, you clothe yourself with your attitude. To wear the proper attire means to have a realistic mindset and mentally prepare for all seasons of life.
- Map. When in doubt during a hike, you can always consult the map. A map can be trusted to help you make the right decisions that will lead you home. Your walk with the Holy Spirit will be consistent with all those who have done it before. The people who walked with Jesus - the embodiment of the Holy Spirit - tell their stories in the Bible, creating a map for us that can be trusted when we are in doubt.

Playing it Safe Never Changed the World

One person bold enough to follow the direction of the Holy Spirit can inspire a movement. Don't be afraid to be the foolish dancer that others make fun of. If you follow the leading of the Holy Spirit and lean upon His strength, you may feel alone for a bit. However, your life can be the inspiration that helps people overcome their personal fears and follow the Holy Spirit's assignment for their lives. Maybe a group of people are simply waiting for someone who is completely surrendered to the Holy Spirit to show them how it's done. People are looking for leaders who lean on the strength of the Holy Spirit.

Never play it safe. People who have influenced eternity are willing to follow the Holy Spirit regardless of their weakness. People who have changed eternity understand that the strength of the Holy Spirit works best in the middle of personal weakness. In our weakness, He is made strong.

CHAPTER TWENTY-TWO

THIS ISN'T WHAT I HAD IN MIND

Our zeal for doing something good can disqualify us from experiencing something great. We're wired to prove our value. Because of that, we're equipped with passion to fuel our work. We believe in ideas and promote them through actions and words. When those ideas become something other than what we expected, it is easy to abandon them and look for something else. Our level of unconditional surrender can be affected by the paradigm of our expectation. Expectation is a strong driver of motivation. Expectation helps us see a glimpse of the future. Expectation can also be our biggest stumbling block to unconditional surrender.

I've used a slogan when directing large events:

Blessed are the flexible, for they will not be bent out of shape.

If I could suggest an addition to the Beatitudes, it would be this one. Great flexibility is needed during unconditional surrender. Stiff expectations and an incorrect paradigm coupled with a zeal for your cause can make it difficult to experience great things God intends for us. Greatness is not always found through passion and commitment; greatness is found through surrender.

The Biggest Letdown of All

The Gospels display the inconsistency of Jesus' disciples. At one moment, they are healing the sick. Other moments, they are fighting for position in the new kingdom Jesus is talking about. The twelve disciples that spent the most time with Jesus missed the significance of His life. The Gospel of John refers to these instances when it says that *"they did not understand what he was saying to them"* and *"after Jesus was glorified, then they remembered."*[10]

These disciples of Jesus were full of passion and believed in the idea of Jesus being a king. They weren't ready to accept the process of how Jesus would be King of Kings. That process would shake their expectations to the core. Only resurrection from the grave convinced some of them who had lost their way. The disciple's story is not that different from our own. Projects begun in zeal have ended in ruins. Relationships begun with deep love have ended with indifference. Even mission work that began with promise has ended in brokenness. If I were a disciple of Jesus and watched Him die on a cross, I would think, "This isn't quite what I had in mind."

---

[10] John 10:6, 12:16 ESV

Resurrection Intent

God could have rescued Jesus from suffering on the cross. He could have sent legions of angels to secure His only son, saving Him from the horrible deeds of men. He didn't, though. Because God did not spare His only Son, we can understand His intent whenever we are faced with something that we didn't have in mind.

The Holy Spirit was the hero during resurrection day. The same Holy Spirit that raised Jesus can live in each one of us. There needed to be a resurrection before the significance of the cross could take effect in our lives. Without that resurrection, the true effect of redemption and indwelling would not have been possible. The resurrection intent of God for the things in your life depends completely and wholly upon your level of personal surrender. If your level of surrender and trust towards God is great, the resurrection effect upon the situations in your life will be powerful.

The Butterfly Effect

It is fascinating how a caterpillar becomes a butterfly. When a caterpillar creates the cocoon, its cellular structure is broken down and transformed into something new.[11] The caterpillar emerges with a completely different identity. There are some parallels in how to deal with the resurrection intent of God in our circumstances.

- <u>The cocoon.</u> A caterpillar must create a cocoon for transformation. This cocoon serves as protection, but

---

[11] http://www.metamorphosisthefilm.com/

it is also designed to facilitate a change. Cocoons are intentional. A person must have a desire for transformation. This cocoon serves as the place where the Holy Spirit is allowed to work deep in the heart. Authenticity is the lining of the cocoon created by a person. Authenticity is most necessary for thorough transformation to take place. Having a place to communicate with the Holy Spirit apart from environmental distractions, daily stresses, and lurking predators is the foundation for becoming unrecognizable.

- The change. A caterpillar's cellular structure changes. It creates an enzyme that melts the caterpillar's body within the cocoon. From that liquid, the butterfly takes shape. A person's inner spiritual makeup has to change. Challenges that were once debilitating must be overcome. Mindsets that used to cause stumbling must be dismissed. The melting occurring within a butterfly is paralleled by the Holy Spirit melting away old trauma, ingrained mindsets, and debilitating fears. What the Holy Spirit brings is a DNA of trust and new perspective. The person must initiate that change. Once initiated, the Holy Spirit brings the power to make the change.
- The perspective. A caterpillar emerging as a butterfly has a different view of the world. From grass roots to treetops, the perspective is broader, higher, and more encompassing. A butterfly will actually retain some of the memories it had as a caterpillar. Those memories do not affect its perspective. A person emerging from a trial or stress has a different view of the world. It can either be a perspective like a butterfly or like a caterpillar. It is sad when a trial or stress comes and goes without teaching anything. How tragic is it when

transformation fails to take place? The perspective a person has when emerging from trouble is related to the choices made in the time of trial. A poor perspective (caterpillar) can come from a misguided expectation. What if a person expected the cocoon to be protective instead of transformative?

The Obstacle to Resurrection

The obstacle to resurrection can present itself when we are closest to the destination. In 1995, I lived in Washington, D.C., for a time during an internship. I lived with a family in the southeast part of the city. I didn't know much about city transportation, so I was told how to take a bus to the subway for a self-guided tour. Getting to my destination was easy with direction. Getting back home without direction became difficult.

After my tour, I didn't know which bus to take after the last subway stop. I jumped on one that had the name of a neighborhood that sounded similar to the one I lived in. Unfortunately, that neighborhood was nowhere near the neighborhood I lived in. Congress Park is not the same as Congress Heights. I rode the entire route until it came to the end of the line. As I waited for the bus to move, the driver looked in his mirror and asked me if I was going to get off the bus. I told him where I needed to go, and he gave me the instructions on how to get there. With his help, I arrived at my destination.

I must have looked out of place sitting on a stationary bus waiting for it to go. That bus wasn't going to move. It wouldn't have mattered if I asked the bus driver to take me to my destination. There was no way I was going to arrive on that bus until I got off and changed transportation lines. The greatest obstacle to the resurrection of dead things in our lives is waiting on a bus that is not going anywhere. Our personal expectation can be the bus we wait on. The expectation we have for a process to be completed can be stuck until we are given a fresh set of directions. An obstacle to resurrection can be a stuck expectation. The bus of our expired expectation will not get us to the destination until we are willing to change mindsets.

Our flexibility and willingness towards obedience will be the qualities that help us change bus (expectation) lines. We cannot get to our destination with the mindset that brings us halfway. The disciples' expectation of Jesus setting up an earthly kingdom had to be changed so they could participate in a heavenly one. With God's plan, the worst possible situation actually turned out to be the best. Because of the work of Jesus and the process He endured, the Holy Spirit is now available to live through us the same way as He did through Jesus. We have to be willing to experience God's resurrection plans so that the Holy Spirit can lead us into the greatness that God has designed for us. Don't let the obstacle of broken expectations stand in your way. Even if things don't turn out the way you hoped for, trust God that He has a better way for you. Most likely, you'll see that the resurrection He designed was much better than the expectation you had hoped for.

CHAPTER TWENTY-THREE

SO THAT'S WHAT IT LOOKS LIKE!

It's hard to see the end of something before the beginning. In hindsight, these are a few things I wish I could have seen the ending before the beginning:
- Driving too fast can cause accidents.
- Frying bacon without a shirt is a bad idea.
- Spending money for things that you want leaves you lacking money for the things you need.
- Kind gestures really do make a difference, even if they don't appear to at first.
- That dream inside of you might make a difference in someone's life. Finish the project.
- Life is like a vapor. Value every moment with those you love and value people with respect.

I wish I could see the big picture all the time. It would be nice to see the ending of something before the beginning. Even when life's vision can be fuzzy, a surrendered person's perspective is always sharper than the ones who are trying to see on their own.

The Magician's Volunteer

I would not be a good assistant for a magician. My family was on vacation, and we happened upon a show. In many cases, a magician will call on someone from the audience to help with the illusion. I don't know how I got picked, but there I was on the stage with the magician. The instructions were simple. Reach inside the box and pull something out. The magic man was so kind to show me how to do it. Unfortunately, his hand came out of the box with a mouse trap on his fingers. There was no way I was going to reach into a box for a mousetrap. I did what any other kid would have done. I ran right off the side, jumped off the stage, and never went back. I'm not certain how he finished that illusion. All I know is that I wasn't in it.

God's Not a Magician

It's difficult to trust God through the illusion of confusing situations. The illusion can be a trial of faith or experience of suffering. Like my volunteer experience with that magician, most of us prefer to take the exit, stage left. Illusions appear real. A good illusion can trick the eyes and send a wrong message to the brain of what reality is. God does not create illusions to confuse us but offers a perspective for us to see reality. He gives us the ability to interpret life's illusions through trust in the Holy Spirit.

Being surrendered to the work of the Holy Spirit will provide perfect vision. The work of the Holy Spirit helps us to see through the illusion of the situation and into the solution.

The Holy Spirit will use time and consistency to help us see clearly.

- Time. People have questions about their walk with God and if He really speaks to them. Other people claim that God is speaking to them about everything. One test to determine if what you are hearing is an illusion or a reality is to give it time. A friend of mine who is a songwriter had a great idea for a song at 3 a.m. only to realize a couple hours later when he woke up how bad that idea was. When in doubt, take a nap. If you think this is something that is worth pursuing, intentionally take some time to let it sink in. If the thought is an illusion, it will dry up under the test of time.
- Consistency. There's a difference between nagging and nudging. The words of the Holy Spirit are always consistent. We'll hear them when we are ready to listen. If you've had a recurring thought to do something and it has come back over the test of time, give it consideration that it might be something of reality and not just the illusion of your own thinking. It could be the next step that God is asking you to take.

The Greatest of These is Love

An example of the work of the Holy Spirit is His love for us. People who love others will do everything to help them. They care deeply about other people. It's the same with the Holy Spirit's work in our lives. There's a reason why we don't always get the full picture or all of the details. We'd more than likely mess something up or be afraid of the magnificence of God's plan for us. God's love for us will provide the ability to see what He is up to in our lives. People who live surrendered lives understand that. They have allowed the love of God to enter their hearts and perfect their hearts. Only the love of God can help us become worthy in God's sight without feeling like we have to do something to earn it.

If you want to know what the plan or purpose for your life is, give God some time to work. Listen closely for the words that come back to you again and again. As you grow in love for God and for others, the purpose will become clear. It won't matter that you don't know the end from the beginning. The love you have from God will carry you through the times when the picture is fuzzy. You'll learn how to be loved. Learning to be loved isn't reflected by the circumstances dealt to you. A difficult life is not a reflection of God's lack of love for you. Learning how to be loved by God is the understanding that His love never changes towards you. It's an honor to accept the love of the Holy Spirit. In essence, it is accepting the very presence of God into your life. The honor of accepting God's love becomes real when you allow God to walk with you in this life.

Dave Donaldson of Convoy of Hope and his brothers, Hal and Steve, lost their father in a car accident. They were children at the time and their family was thrust into poverty almost overnight. Members of their church were quick to help the Donaldsons. One family went the extra mile and invited them to live in their home as they began to rebuild their lives. Years later, in Dave's book, *The Compassion Revolution*, he described the moment when his family went to live in their new home. As the family was walking up the sidewalk, the father of the house opened the door to them and said, "Welcome to your new home. You are now with family."

Accepting God's love is simply giving Him that opportunity to work within you and live with you. You're with family.

This is What it Looks Like

Details of the journey are not a deal breaker to the surrendered heart. The last act of the play does not need to be spelled out before the production begins. People with surrendered hearts trust the Holy Spirit to design and implement the very plan created for them to do. Surrendered people realize the big picture is something they are part of. Their confidence believes in God's ability to complete things. They understand the meaning of pain through trials. They do a great job of keeping things in perspective and giving God time to work in the situation. The work of the Holy Spirit is very active in their lives.

Un-surrendered people have a difficult time with this. They want to see what happens before they obey. They also want to be assured of their safety before taking a risk. In many cases, they spend way too much time trying to fix something that God needs time to work on. Un-surrendered people look at the circumstances around them; God is trying to help them see the circumstances within them.

A person with a surrendered heart never has a vision problem. They are confident walking the path in front of them. They trust God to bring them through the difficulties they face. In many cases, you'll never see them break their stride. Their trust in God will bring them through any temporary illusion and into eternal reality. For them, their surrender helps them see what everything looks like through God's perspective.

CHAPTER TWENTY-FOUR

FEARLESS AGRESSION

During my high school wrestling career, I wrestled the perfect match in January of 1992. A loss in mid-December fueled my intensity to win the match in January. My opponent was from Greenbush, MN, a small town in northern Minnesota that was known for the quality of its wrestling program. As a team, we had never beaten them, but I had no fear going into this match. Nervousness was replaced with focus. I wasn't worried about becoming tired or making a mistake. My focus was on execution and finishing. The match was one-sided. At one point late in the first period, my opponent looked over to his coaches and shrugged his shoulders. There was nothing he could do and nothing his coaches could say to help him. Early in the second period I pinned him and won the match.

Against an opponent with little experience, I expected this type of match. He was two years younger than me, so I didn't know what he was capable of or what his potential would be. Years later when I traveled to Greenbush as a fan, I discovered what type of wrestler my opponent had become. During his senior year, he wrestled his way to the championship round of the state finals. He placed second in the state of Minnesota. My state wrestling fortunes were not so kind. The highest I placed was fourth.

The match I wrestled in January indicated my potential if my focus had been consistent. I had no fear of losing or becoming fatigued and wasn't even focused on the end result. My focus was glued to my ability to wrestle well. I let the end result take care of itself; I focused on what I could do in the moment.

The fearless aggression that changes the evil systems in this world can be traced to an unwavering focus on the work of the Holy Spirit. When I focus on the Holy Spirit's work, the presence of God is revealed in my life. My trust makes way for the results of the Holy Spirit. The perspective of a surrendered heart is the confidence of God's work being completed in each situation. With a perspective of God's work being real and active, what does a person really have to lose?

Getting Back on the Horse

Athletes think any physical activity is easy. Even if you've never tried something before, it certainly can't be that difficult. I thought that when I tried to ride a skateboard and wound up with a broken leg and ankle. Skateboarding is one sport that I'll leave to the professionals.

There are some things in life that cannot be left to the professionals. Situations that have broken emotions, twisted mindsets, or caused physical harm can create a pause in the progress of life. The unresolved issues of pain and destruction can cause people to give up on their dreams, hesitate when they need to move forward, and give in to pressure. During those times, people might defer to others to change the brokenness of the world. The only person that can offer the solution you were born with is you. No one else can present what you have to offer. So what do you do when you're afraid to try again?

Redirect the Fear

Running is a great defense. Pain is a wonderful communicator. Stepping back in a crowd can protect you from being a volunteer. Fear can preserve life. But fear can strangle life too. The fear of danger and loss can prevent a person from fully living. Since it can be difficult to avoid fear, it is good to redirect the fear in a healthy way such as focusing on what you can do in the moment and to stop worrying about an end result you cannot control.

The fearless aggression of a surrendered heart does not consider loss in normal ways. To the surrendered heart, everything is loss compared to the ability to know the heart of God. What really matters when compared to being secured in the love of God? Within the surrendered heart is the unending message of God's faithfulness and His ability to redeem all of life's painful situations.

How Would I Think Differently?

A surrendered heart has thoughts like these:
- <u>I can embrace a challenge.</u> The challenge I face may be stacked with the odds of failure. No problem. I understand what my role is when working with the Holy Spirit. Within that challenge, I am unafraid to fail. As I address the challenge, I may be confronted

with the reality of dealing with success that comes with a victory. The Holy Spirit will teach me how to handle success.

- <u>I trust God's leading in my life.</u> God is driving the vehicle of my life. My journey is directed by the Holy Spirit. Even if the destination seems far away, I know that God will lead me there. When I truly understand and embrace this perspective, I can give all of my effort to what is in front of me whether I like that part of the journey or not. I know that the Holy Spirit knows me best and is equipping me with the qualities I'll need.
- <u>I understand that pain may be part of the process.</u> Pain means something different to me when I surrender. Pain is not pleasant, but it can be productive. What I focus on determines my personal growth through pain. I can focus on getting rid of the pain, or I can focus on allowing God to work in the middle of the pain. My pain does not separate me from the Holy Spirit; it serves as a reason to draw me closer.
- <u>I'm not afraid to fail in trying something new.</u> With a surrendered heart, I don't make decisions based on calculated successes. I don't worry about failing because it shows me how *not* to do something. If I have the chance to experience something bigger than me or participate in an opportunity that scares me to death, I take it. I embrace the moment because the Holy Spirit brought me here. What good is trusting in God only during times of safety? The giants I face are nothing in comparison to the power at work within me.

Perfected Love

I knew an individual whose father cared little for him. Throughout the son's life, those wounds motivated his actions and thoughts towards others. Bravado replaced confidence, and desire for acceptance ruled his behavior. Insecurity posed as strength. Through the masks, you could see the pain.

Life is hard when you're unsure of your foundation. When the foundation of life is built upon performance or a desire for acceptance, everything we do to gain what we most desire is like chasing the wind. Love is the greatest power on this earth. It is who God is and is the essence of the Holy Spirit. Imagine if you were able to love God with the exact love that He loves you with? This love cannot be earned no matter the effort. This love cannot be lost regardless of the offense.

A good way to determine what your foundation is built on is to evaluate your view towards God. Do you strive for an imagined acceptance? Are you fearful of knowing Him in a deeper way? Can you trust Him with your deepest secrets? Every question can find the answer in our acceptance of His love. The question is not if God loves us; it is if we have embraced His love without offering a reason for Him to do so.

The reason I'm able to risk it all is because I don't have a thing to prove. I've already accepted what He proved for me on the cross. The Holy Spirit is the down payment of God's deposit of love towards us. The Spirit is the evidence of God's love on this earth. I simply have to sign the document of my heart, opening it up for the Holy Spirit to love me.

Love creates courage in people. What others see as a risk, people with surrendered hearts see as an opportunity to return God's love back to Him. Love covers a multitude of offenses. While some people may be extremely irritable and impatient towards others, those who have accepted God's love see through the actions and into the heart. They understand the motivation. Those who have been perfected by God's love are fearless and aggressive in their surrender to Him. They know they may lack everything for their assignment, but they follow their faith because of God's ability to supply. They know that God's love is the cornerstone of their confidence and nothing can ever change that. These are the people that change the world. This type of fearless aggression fueled by love influences others and motivates generations.

CHAPTER TWENTY-FIVE

GO THROUGH THE FIRE

Wrestling is intense for participants and spectators. A year after college graduation, I had the opportunity to help coach my brother's wrestling team. My friend John and I were always at the matches as spectators. During a tournament, one of our wrestlers had a tough opponent as well an incompetent referee. We weren't shy about vocalizing our opinions loud and clear. All throughout the match, John's anger level was rising because of the ref's calls. At one point, his frustration boiled over, and in his outdoor voice he yelled, "Ref, you suck!" It just happened to be right in the middle of a transition in the match when the entire gymnasium was quiet. Point delivered, point taken, and laughter ensued.

I can't remember if our wrestler won the match or not. What I do remember is how we felt in the middle of that contest. The part of our soul that feels things is one of our strongest motivators. It's hard to be zealous for something that you don't care about. It's also hard to manage emotions once they're running over a situation. A perspective of unconditional surrender allows you to identify what moves you and focus that zeal on changing something you care about for the good.

Fiery Zeal

The Pentecostal movement began in Los Angeles in 1906. People who were the early pioneers of this experience participated in church services that produced signs and wonders. Attendees experienced the presence of God for extended periods. Others were healed. People repented of the sin they harbored in their hearts. The emphasis on the work of the Holy Spirit is the trademark of my Pentecostal church history.

With that history, I've experienced things that have been out of control. I've been in meetings where spontaneous laughter erupted, gold dust was discovered, and people fell on the ground. On the flip side, I've also experienced some deep moments with God during an altar call at the end of a service. Part of my journey has been discovering the type of fire that lasts and makes the biggest difference. Concerning this fire, I've come to the conclusions that this spiritual zeal isn't intended for an expression of exuberance in a safe setting among saints; it's intended for a demonstration of miraculous light in the darkest areas.

The Other Aspect of Fire

Fire changes things to ash. It consumes material and transforms it. I've seen house fires, tree fires, tire fires, trash fires, and grass fires. It's all the same: hot, smoky, and mesmerizing. It's hard not to look at a fire when it's burning. It's easy to miss an important aspect of fire when we dismiss the ash it produces. Ash is more than a simple byproduct of fire. One characteristic of ash is that it can be moved by the wind. Being moved by the Holy Spirit is preceded by experiencing the fire of the Holy Spirit. The purpose of fire from the Holy Spirit is to enhance obedience, not just provide an exciting experience.

Fire Extinguishers

If the fire of the Holy Spirit transforms our lives, we choose how much of that fire burns within us. There are extinguishers to put the fire out. You should be aware of these fire extinguishers so you don't extinguish the Holy Spirit's fire within your life.

- The extinguisher of unmet expectations. This extinguisher is used when your expectations of a vision are not met. You might have had something in mind during a process, but it took a different turn. The change in direction can leave you disillusioned or disappointed. Unmet expectations keep you from adding fuel to the fire.
- The extinguisher of disappointment. Closely related to the extinguisher of unmet expectations, this is when the emotion of the moment seizes control of the situation. Disappointment follows disillusionment with a sense of finality. The outcome you hoped for is not happening. The dream is dead. The outcome has been sabotaged by someone else. There is no hope. Disappointment is like water on a fire, leaving nothing but stinky, smoky remains.
- The extinguisher of misaligned perspective. This happens when long, intense focus is placed on the wrong thing. Misaligned focus can be changed by a simple shift of view. Misaligned perspective happens when someone clings to their own perspective, giving no

room for the Holy Spirit's perspective. Instead of seeing the entire picture, only a piece of the picture is seen. Without the full picture, it appears that there's nothing left to burn. You're out of fuel.

How We Know What is Important

Transformed people care about other people. Their hearts beat with compassion towards others without hope. Jesus wasn't moved simply because people needed help. He was moved because they needed leadership. They needed to make empowered decisions that would provide stability, security, and hope. The fire of the Holy Spirit can change our thinking from labeling people with entitlement issues (even if they exhibit them) to seeing past those issues and into the potential that person contains.

Transformed people redeem suffering and don't seek escape from it. This doesn't mean they like to suffer; they simply don't try to avoid pain at all costs. They know that life is full of uncertainty, and they hold onto it loosely. They don't attempt to build mindsets that guarantee tranquility; they trust that even when they suffer, the Holy Spirit will redeem the situation. They realize that suffering always comes before resurrection. Dead things cannot come back to life without being buried.

Transformed people come to the end of themselves quickly. They don't lack inner strength. They simply know how to stop trying so hard so that the Holy Spirit can work in their lives. They know how to get out of the way. Struggling within situations instead of accepting God's help is an effort in futility. Transformed people realize the value, worth, and dignity of others. They don't have a problem putting others first. Coming in second is not being the first loser. In their mind, second place finishes bring first place rewards.

The Fire of Desire

If the Holy Spirit burns within me, my choices become *want-to* instead of *have-to*. I choose the work of the Holy Spirit over a religious obligation. Choosing the work of the Holy Spirit multiplies the experience and obedience within my life. This is not a struggle once you've turned to ash. The slightest nudge can move you to the place the Holy Spirit directs you to. You won't need a wind storm to get your attention; you'll be in tune to the breath of God.

CHAPTER TWENTY-SIX

THE GLASS IS ALWAYS HALF-FULL

A surrendered person is an eternal optimist. Their optimism is fueled by the tenacious perspective of possibility. Tony and Antoinette's life began like many others in their neighborhood. Antoinette was raised in a broken home with abuse, drugs, and alcohol, and Tony's family also experienced drug and alcohol influences. They met, married, and began their lives together. Antoinette said, "I was looking to be rescued out of my situation and into anything better than was currently being offered."

Tony worked hard but was involved in moving narcotics and was always selling something. When they had a baby and an apartment to pay for, Tony's sales in the South Phoenix drug industry began to climb. An outsider would never think that Tony was a player on the drug scene. During this time in their lives, they had everything they wanted. Antoinette remembers that by the time she was eighteen, they had a fully furnished house, multiple vehicles, and a great life.

In 1996, Tony's brother and cousin were involved in a triple homicide. A father, a mother, and a daughter died. Because of those killings, the neighborhood became a war zone as families fought one another. Drive-by shootings became a daily occurrence. After some time, the situation calmed but was still brewing beneath the surface. It wasn't over.

Tony and Antoinette hosted a family wedding in the backyard of their home. That night, during the wedding, tragedy struck. The other family retaliated and shot nine people. Antoinette recalls seeing her cousin, who was pregnant, die from a gunshot wound to the head. Watching her cousin die was one of the hardest things she ever faced.

Soon after that, Tony and Antoinette moved out of South Phoenix to Avondale. It was at this point that their marriage hit rock bottom. They didn't know how they were going to make it work, but God was at work. God began speaking to Antoinette about bringing the kids to church. As a family, they tried out a couple of churches in their area, but it "just wasn't working for them." There was one more church right across the corner from their house, and Antoinette decided to give it a try. Antoinette and her kids began attending Cornerstone Christian Center, and God began working on her heart. He began speaking to her about forgiving her enemies and the people who had brought her pain. She soon accepted Christ, was baptized in water, and was filled with the Holy Spirit.

In October of 2001, Tony was still dealing drugs to make a living. One day, Antoinette woke up to see a young kid holding a shotgun to her head. Tony placed his hand on her and told her, "These people are going to take what they want and then they will leave. Don't cry." For the next two and a half hours, they hit and kicked Tony and took everything of value in the house. After that, Antoinette told Tony that he needed to stop dealing drugs. It was time for change.

The following Sunday as she was getting ready for church, Tony got ready too. She asked him what he was doing, and he said he was going to church. After a couple of weeks, Tony accepted Christ. As time passed, he felt like a hypocrite because he was still selling drugs to make ends meet while going to church and professing a faith in God. As God dealt with his heart, Tony quit the drug business. The next couple of months would be a financial test. It became a walk of faith.

Slowly but surely, everything they had ever bought with drug money was gone, including their friends. Tony and Antoinette had been the pulse of the party in their previous life, but once their lives changed, so did their friends. With both of them working honest jobs, it was difficult to make ends meet. They needed God to intervene, and He did, but not in the way they prayed for.

Both of them began feeling a call to preach. God was showing them His heart and instilling a call to reach people. When all the earthly distractions had been removed, they heard God's voice clearly. As they responded to that call, they began to lead a small group in their church. People came to their group by the droves and many people accepted Christ. As they continued serving, they felt compelled to start a church. At first, Tony wanted no part of it even though he knew God was speaking to them. They finally said yes to that call and approached their pastor, Rich Brown. He supported them and said they could invite anyone they wanted within the congregation to join them in the new church plant. Ten people committed to join them and they began training and preparing to launch their church. They were going back to South Phoenix, to the neighborhood that had caused them so much pain.

Antoinette remembers the struggle she had in moving back:

> *It wasn't easy coming back here because of all the pain we had felt years prior. When we moved back and I was looking for homes, we could see that the neighborhood had changed. We eventually looked at a house in the*

> very neighborhood that we had come from, next to 16th Street and Southern Avenue. As I was driving through the neighborhood, which I remembered as the war zone, I was thinking that there was no way I could bring my kids here. I saw the house we were considering to rent and noticed the family across the street sitting in their yard, drinking 40's and listening to Tupac. A few houses from ours, I saw another place that they would bring illegal immigrants. I told God, "I know you want me to do this but I can't. There are just too many hurts! I want to be obedient but look at this place!" God then spoke to my heart and said, "Remember when you lived in the house on that corner? I saved you, didn't I?"

As their church, New Destiny, was being launched, word got out in the neighborhood that Tony Rodriguez was coming back to pastor a new church. The people in the community were incredulous. They could hardly believe that a guy who once was a drug dealer was now a pastor and coming back to the neighborhood. People would approach Tony just to see if it was true. Antoinette remembers the interactions. "They would leave those conversations knowing that if God could do something in Tony's life like that, He could certainly work in theirs."

Other people were amazed that Tony had no fear coming back to the streets. Tony told people "One day, even my enemies will come back and shake my hand." Today, New Destiny's focus is rebuilding the family structure in the community. Healthy families make healthy communities. Healed people make whole communities.

The Best Possibilities are the Ones that Require Endurance

In 2010, Forbes magazine published an article about why wrestlers make the best employees. The author's opinion (and mine) is that a wrestler is used to facing adversity. When athletes in other sports are done with practice or a game, they can focus their attention on other things in life. Not so with a wrestler. He must constantly submit himself to eating properly in order to make the weight of his class. During practices, he has to improve his technique, endurance, and strength to be prepared for the contest. When one match is over, he has to repeat the cycle to get ready for the next. The cycle of endurance is one that a wrestler learns in order to win.

Tony and Antoinette are people who tenaciously embraced the possible. Through God touching their lives and delivering them, they answered the call of God to go back into a tough neighborhood. They wrestle with challenges daily in planting a church, but because of the work that God performed in their lives, they have the perspective that God is able to do anything. I've been in their neighborhood. Most people drive around it. The only thing that can change the atmosphere of that community is the presence of God.

People who practice surrendering their lives to God live with an expectation of possibility. They trust the Holy Spirit is working on their behalf and on things they are unaware of. Through the work of the Holy Spirit, they have overcome. For those who struggle with a positive perspective, consider the possibility that God can bring in the middle of the most negative circumstance. You may not see the end result of what God is going to do. However, you can be a part of expecting the possibility by tenaciously holding on to the work that only the Holy Spirit can do. Your perspective on the possible will be proportionate with your surrender to the work of the Holy Spirit. All things are possible.

CHAPTER TWENTY-SEVEN

WHAT REALLY MATTERS

The "non-profit" institution neither supplies goods or services nor controls. It's "product" is neither a pair of shoes nor an effective regulation. Its product is a changed human being. The non-profit institutions are human-change agents. Their "product" is a cured patient, a child that learns, a young man or woman grown into a self-respecting adult; a changed human life altogether.

Peter Drucker[12],

To me, this was the most meaningful statement from the book. It was written in the introduction before mission, performance, leadership, or management were discussed. This statement is the life mission of a surrendered individual. Surrendered lives produce changed lives. Surrendered people help others realize there is more to life than the mundane. Surrender creates the influence of the Holy Spirit to change people into His image. The greatest works are difficult to measure. Recipients of life-changing works do not always

---

[12] Managing the Non Profit Organization

vocalize what has happened to them. They simply live it, and we sometimes never know about it.

Surrendered living reinforces the perspective that people matter. People are God's most valuable resource on the planet. When other things become more important than the life of a person whom God loves deeply, the craziest things get excessive emphasis. If you want to change the world, understand what really matters to God. Being surrendered to the Holy Spirit will get you on track. The moment you begin to embrace the perspective of what really matters to God, be prepared for distractions to emerge.

Extreme Effort

I was a member of the wrestling team during my first semester of college. I learned that the power of focus can make a difference in performance. The week after Thanksgiving, I came back from vacation eleven pounds over the weight I had to make in four days. It was going to take a monumental effort to reach my weight goal and compete in the weekend tournament. Making my weight class meant that I would need to focus night and day on making weight.

It wasn't hard to focus during practice; I had colleagues and coaches to help me with the drills and competition. Focus was a challenge when I was by myself, right before meals, and in class. On Thursday evening, the night before weigh-in, I hardly slept because I knew I had a goal to meet the following morning and I was dying of thirst. On Friday morning, a couple of hours before the official weigh-in, I was still two pounds overweight. I had two hours. Those two hours were long and lonely. Sitting in the sauna feels like an eternity when you have to reach a goal.

Right before our official weigh-in, I reached my goal and made the weight. I've never forgotten that experience because it showed me that intense focus is needed to change something that appears impossible. Very few people lose eleven pounds in four days to compete in a difficult tournament. Even fewer extend the effort to embrace what really matters when they are trying to change their world. When you surrender your heart, what seems impossible is completely doable when your focus is fixed on what God can do rather than what you're trying to do.

Ignoring the Bright and Shiny

Distraction is the archenemy to focus. We'll never be able to eliminate distractions. Our goal is to remain focused on what matters. As long as evil has room to work on the earth, distractions will remain.

To focus, understand these principles:

- See the end from the beginning. Understand that God is maneuvering you to a place where He wants you to be. When it appears that you're losing it all, God is probably helping you sift through the things that don't matter. The earthly thing you lose might be the thing that needs to be replaced with something eternal.
- The counterfeit often precedes the authentic. When you ask God for something in your life, there is a chance that a good opportunity will arrive and pose as the answer to your prayers. Don't jump at the first thing that comes your way; it might be a distraction. Give it the test of time. Ask the Holy Spirit if this is authentic or if it is

counterfeit. If it is the real deal, you'll embrace the opportunity with peace. If there's no peace, there should be no action.
- <u>You have to let things go.</u> You need to have a loose grip on temporary things in order to embrace divine opportunities. Let go of trouble, personal goals, and deep desires of your heart. God knows all these things; you can't hold on to things and expect them to get fixed if you can't trust God with them. Distractions come easily when trust in the Holy Spirit is non-existent. Remember: God's got this.

What Really Matters

One reason the devil creates distractions is to blind the eyes of people and make them ineffective in loving others. The way to truly live is to truly love. Surrendered hearts know what it means to love God first, others second, and their own lives third.

People who are written about are often considered a little crazy. They're not crazy, just full of perspective of what really matters. Who would sell a family farm in order to pursue a call to enter another country, learn another language, and build churches? Who would give the shoes off of his feet to the one who had none of his own? Who would teach in a school system abandoned by others and labeled as failing? Who would spend their lives helping young people find their dreams while forsaking their own? Who would build systems of rescue to free humans from trafficking? Who would willingly give away a fortune if it meant that kids could go to sleep with food in their stomachs? Who would give his life as a ransom for many in order that all could experience the opportunity to be sons and daughters of God? Every single person who has done these things and more realized that God values people.

Practicing the End in Mind Mentality

Peter Drucker continues his thoughts about non-profits functioning as agents of change: "The non-profit institution is not merely delivering a service. It wants the end use to be not a user but a doer." The best end-in-mind strategy is to experience the power of the Holy Spirit with other people. Surrendered hearts are ineffective when isolated. God's value system asks those who have been impacted by His Spirit to make a difference for someone else. As long as they are willing to reach beyond their own lives, the Holy Spirit will do the rest.

Keep these things in mind when working towards the future:

- God wants all people to know Him. God's wants all people to know His salvation. People who have surrendered their hearts to the value system of the Holy Spirit realize this. Those who haven't realized this are surrendered to the desires of their own value system. That system usually keeps people thinking only about themselves.
- God cares about character. No matter what we do for God, it pales in comparison to who God wants us to become. Who we are is the foundation for what we do. What we do doesn't create our identity. The condition of our heart creates our identity. When God transforms the deepest part of our lives, a perspective shift comes naturally.

- We can't make Him love us more than He already does. People who practice living with the end in mind understand God's great love. They don't strive for God's acceptance. They know their acceptance and live confidently in His love.
- The practice of listening influences future direction. This is the practice of focus. People who practice the end-in-mind perspective constantly focus on the value system of the Holy Spirit. Over time, their focus skills mature with the help of the Holy Spirit. They understand that God will speak to them and direct their steps.

CHAPTER TWENTY-EIGHT

TREASURE IN CLAY JARS

You might live in a small town if something is no sooner done than said. Someone once said that if you live in a small town and don't want something talked about, you'd best not do it. If you grew up in a small town, you know several things to be true:
- Your schoolteachers probably had your parents in their class.
- It might be an hour to the nearest McDonalds.
- Your town might have one stoplight.
- When one family goes through hardship, other people will help them.
- Neighbors aren't the people that live next door; they are the people in your community.

People in small towns understand the community and the value of people. While people in a small town may recognize the value of someone else, the surrendered person recognizes the value of people wherever they are. Their perspective is that all people carry value.

The Art of Community

Sixty years ago, life was different than it is today. People worked on their farms and lived within a couple miles of each other. Near our farmstead in North Dakota, there were many families. Today there are only two. Today's community is not always based upon distance. It is based upon relationships and perspective. A person surrendered to the work of the Holy Spirit can be instrumental in creating community. More so, they affirm the dignity of the individuals who make up the community. Honoring individual dignity builds community.

Treasure Hunters

I've never been good at finding things. During a Newlywed Game, my wife said about me, "He doesn't lose things, but he can't find anything." And that's why I'll never be a gold miner. In the mid 1800s, many people left everything for the gold rush in California. They traveled over land and around continents for a chance to strike it rich. Those who helped build the mining camps profited from goods sold to the miners and prospectors. Villains robbed and killed people for their gold. The few who did strike it rich became the poster children for those wishing for a better life. People who were willing to risk it all sometimes ended up losing it all. God defines earthly treasure differently. The most valuable resource to Him is people. Those who surrender their lives to the work of the Holy Spirit see people in the same way.

Oskar Schindler demonstrated the value of a human soul when he spent his fortune protecting the Jews from Adolph Hitler during World War II. Schindler was initially interested in making profit from his business. His value system shifted once his Jewish employees were in danger of being imprisoned in concentration camps. Late in the movie *Shindler's List*, Schindler laments not saving more people. If he had sold his watch, he could have saved more people. Similar objects could have rescued others. That scene illustrates the value God places on people. Treasure on earth doesn't compare with the treasure of people.

When a person sees resources as God sees them, their value system changes to reflect eternal values. Human resources only get better with use. When people reflect the dignity and image of their Creator, incredible value is displayed.

The IMAGE of God

My perspective through the lens of a surrendered heart looks at people a little differently. I don't see ways in which they can be used for my benefit. I don't see people in all of their weaknesses. I see in them the potential that the Holy Spirit has designed for them. I see them in His IMAGE.

- I – Intelligent. God has created people with a sense to think and make choices for themselves. They have the opportunity to choose between life and death, living for themselves or living for God. Because they have the choice of whom they will serve, they need to make the choice for themselves. Their decisions can be more influenced by my love for them than my ability to change their thinking. A renewed mind is a product of the Holy Spirit, not of my persuasion.

- M – Motivated. Not all people exhibit this trait. Laziness is an enemy to motivation. Unmotivated people are broken people. The Holy Spirit heals and restores broken things. When people accept forgiveness and a right relationship with God, their motivation is for others to experience that same forgiveness and restoration. It only takes a moment to motivate. With that motivation, an entire movement can be sustained. Through surrender, people are filled with potential and motivation to change the world.

- A – Aspiring. Aspiring people are growing people. The Holy Spirit helps people grow into the design that God intends for their lives. They look for ways to develop their character and become more like Jesus. The Holy Spirit transforms people who focus on Him. Growth is the byproduct of the Holy Spirit's influence.
- G – Generous. With the help of the Holy Spirit, every single person can become a giver. God gave His son, the prince of Heaven, to live with us and create a pathway to God's holiness. The Holy Spirit can change people into givers that glorify God and help others see the value in people. A generous heart accepts complete forgiveness and understands how much they have been given. They realize everything they have is a gift from God.
- E – Encouraging. Confident people encourage others. People who have experienced the stability of God's love reflect it well. They no longer have to worry about pleasing God with their efforts; they understand that God's love for them cannot be changed. They return God's love back to Him through the expression of loving others. Even if people are haters and spitefully use other people, the potential for them to reflect the image of God is always there, as long as they are alive. Though the lens of a surrendered heart, I see the

value of a person even if they do not exhibit traits that I admire.

See God's Perspective

Because I see people as God sees them, I work to build them up. I work to help them discover the image they were created in. I love them as I love myself. I understand the power of leading with influence. I know that if I can help them make a decision that empowers their will, heart, and mind towards truly surrendering to the Holy Spirit, they will continue their journey with God. If I violate any part of their image in trying to get what I want from them, they will eventually do the thing they want to do. That's why I cannot use the Holy Spirit as a battering ram in their lives. I have to be intentional about persuading people that the Holy Spirit is Someone to be chosen, not forced upon them.

If I don't see people the way God sees them, I probably have issues with my perspective. Only the Holy Spirit can give me the right perspective towards others. If I think of others as beneath me or try to exert my superiority over them, my perspective is off and needs to be realigned. Other people can see how you view them. Work with the Holy Spirit on this. Get your perspective in order and you will see God work through you and how He values people.

The only thing you can take with you into eternity is the influence you've had on other people. Let God show you how much He values others and allow the Holy Spirit to adjust your focus to match God's perspective.

CHAPTER TWENTY-NINE

iCARE

It was August of 2013 in San Benito, Texas. A woman working in the prayer tent overcame her shyness and prayed with many people. After the event, she was ecstatic. Holding up a small bundle of forms, she said that she had never been able to share her faith in Jesus until today. Today she met new friends by praying with them and is intent upon building relationships with them. Embracing courage, she overcame fear and found new friends. When the Holy Spirit has room to work in our hearts, we see other people differently. We care for others like God cares for them. Our perspective changes, our attitudes are adjusted and our actions help others. In short, we carry the compassion of Christ with us to make a difference in the world.

If Compassion is so Great, Why is it so Difficult?

Caring for people is difficult. It wouldn't be so difficult if people would behave themselves and be a little more teachable. Because we are people, we need to understand that the work of the Holy Spirit helps us truly care for others and overcome these common obstacles:

- <u>Being taken advantage of.</u> I resent being taken advantage of. People may take advantage of your kindness. Con artists prey on good-hearted people. I've been there and know the feeling of being swindled. It's not fun.
- <u>Dealing with drama.</u> Other people's drama is messy. Being involved with other people means that you might get some mud on you from time to time. We are messy. Relationships are messy. Helping people is messy.
- <u>Feeling too busy.</u> You may feel you don't have room for one more relationship. Loving other people is inconvenient. You might be busier than most people, but you always have room for some type of influence.
- <u>Feeling overwhelmed trying to fix other people's problems.</u> Can't they do this on their own? Yes, they can once they gain the instruction they need. Some people don't know where to begin cleaning up the mess their lives have become. They need someone to tell them clearly, without condemnation, how to overcome the obstacles they face.

When facing these obstacles, remember this; you can't do for someone what only he or she can do for themselves. But, sometimes the only way to help people do something for their lives is by influencing them with compassion.

Who Qualifies for My Care?

Jesus was the perfect example of caring for others. He looked for the outcasts, the reviled, the forgotten, and the young. He loved every person, but certain folks received a little bit more of His attention. Jesus found the forgotten. His relationship with God the Father enabled Him to remove all ambition of personal gain and focus on the people that really mattered to God. All people matter to God, but those cast aside by others are the ones He loves to rescue.

The only time we can be like Jesus is when the Holy Spirit is given the ability to work out our security, our identity, and our priority. We cannot care for the least of these if we are pursuing the best things for ourselves. The perspective of an unconditionally surrendered life is one that finds the forgotten.

How the Holy Spirit Changes Me

The Holy Spirit changes my perspective from a capital *I* to a lowercase *i*. He doesn't wave a wand and change us immediately; there is a process that we can experience that will change us for good. The benefits of this process are manifold:

- When I trust the Holy Spirit, self-preservation is minimized. We look out for ourselves when we fear harm or experience insecurity. Self-preservation is strongest among the injured. Self-preservation does not have to be the priority of my life when I trust the Holy Spirit to sustain me.
- When I trust the Holy Spirit, it's easy to set boundaries in relationships. People full of mercy often get taken advantage of because of their good hearts. Intentional boundaries should be set. Merciful people and approval-seeking people have difficulty setting boundaries. If I trust the Holy Spirit for my significance, I won't have to

worry about finding that approval or significance from others. My worth is anchored in the value system of the Holy Spirit.
- <u>When I trust the Holy Spirit, I can love others like God loves me.</u> The love of God is poured into my heart by the Holy Spirit. When the Holy Spirit has room to work in us, God's love is present. Giving access to the Holy Spirit is creating space for Him to work. The things I focus on, spend time with, and think about are access points that influence my thoughts, actions, and words. If I give God those access points, His love will help me to love others deeply.

One Thing to Keep in Mind

Any expression of the Holy Spirit should express a love for others. Words, actions, or deeds without God's love are fraudulent expressions of the Holy Spirit. You'll have to test your own intentions and the actions of other people to determine if the Holy Spirit is working through you. Let love be the barometer of a surrendered life and you'll see things very clearly.

You'll See a Difference

As the Holy Spirit works in you, transformation will take place. The uppercase *I* will begin to change to a lowercase *i* as you embrace God's intentions for other people. You'll begin to see this happening in your life when you find yourself caring for building up, and empowering others.
- <u>iCare.</u> My parents picked up a hitchhiking couple, and they ended up staying with us for two months. The two months that Dave and Pam stayed with our fami-

ly are sure to remain with them for the rest of their lives. When we care, we give God access points to touch other hearts through our kindness and generosity.

- **iBuild.** Relationships are the foundations of transformation. My wife Natalie met a customer at Starbucks years ago. She keeps in touch with her and sends her notes of encouragement from time to time. The relationship has been a mutual building benefit for both parties. Natalie's encouragement during one of their meetings helped express God's love for her friend in a powerful way. Her friend's coaching abilities helped Natalie see another side of her business that she has developed. God uses relationships to build both parties. Without relationships, it's hard to build people.
- **iEmpower.** Encouragement with application builds confidence. Coaches understand this role well. They are not seeking a following; they are trying to build a movement of empowered athletes. Our high school football team had suffered an embarrassing defeat, and we expected the worst in practice the following week. Much to our surprise and ultimately to our encouragement, our coach told us that we were a good team and that we could beat our next opponent. Those words alone helped us finish the year strong and proud of our efforts. Sometimes, it's the small word that helps change the destiny of another person. We empower people with the words we say.

The perspective of an unconditional surrendered heart is focused towards helping people. If you don't have that perspective yet, give God some time and create access points for His Spirit to influence you. You'll find that He's willing to make a change in you and to work incredible change through you.

CHAPTER THIRTY

HERE WE GO

From now on, this is your biggest question: How much influence does the Holy Spirit have in you? The second question is almost as important; How much of that influence are you sharing with the world?

Influence is built upon surrender. Jesus told the disciples to expect a domineering type of leadership when dealing with the insecure leaders of this world. We are not called to that type of leadership. We are called to influence people at their deepest core. We are called to tap into the "want to" of others and help them discover the Holy Spirit's direction. You'll never have to coerce someone to do something through influence. They'll either make the choice or they won't.

Your influence is going to depend upon your willingness to surrender. It will depend upon your perspective through the Holy Spirit. Your influence will be measured by the obstacles you are willing to overcome. It will be strengthened by the mindset you adopt.

Measuring Tools

You'll encounter people who talk about being influenced by the Holy Spirit. You'll find that some of them know what they are talking about while others are talking about a feeling they received by encountering the Holy Spirit. You can know the difference. Evidence of the Holy Spirit's work is demonstrated in these areas. When you surrender to the daily work of the Spirit, you'll develop these attributes:

- Fruitfulness. The fruit of the Spirit will be on display in your life. Love, joy, peace, patience, kindness, goodness, faithfulness, gentleness, and self-control—nothing on this earth can limit the expression of these attributes. The only thing that limits this evidence of the Holy Spirit is an unwillingness to surrender. I believe that actions defined by the fruit of the Spirit would change the world.
- Boldness. The evidence of the Holy Spirit involves boldness. When you have nothing left to lose, your fear has nothing left to stand upon. Why would you be afraid to lose anything when you've already given it all away? Bold people are not necessarily the loudest; they are the most resolute. They carry themselves with reverence for God and do not fear personal loss.
- Zeal. The product of the Holy Spirit is zeal. Caring for something, having a passion towards something, and doing something about it are what zeal is made of. You do have to be careful that you don't get carried away with zeal. Cause and mission can take on a life of their own if not guided by the Holy Spirit. However, zeal is produced when you are aligned with the Holy Spirit. The zeal you carry is an inner fire that

burns white hot. It's not just about being noisy; it's about being effective.
- Wisdom. Thought processes of the Holy Spirit involve wisdom. Seeing the end from the beginning is not a product of systematic thinking. It is a gift of sight from the Holy Spirit. Wisdom given from God cannot be matched by human efforts. Wisdom isn't defined by quantity of study or intellectual activity. Wisdom is about discerning the mind of God for a certain situation.
- Supernatural power. The evidence of the Holy Spirit involves the supernatural. There will be things you cannot explain. You will say things that you never knew were in you. Your prayer life will be more effective. Being able to say something that another person was thinking, sharing a word of encouragement that lifts someone up during a dark time, and watching a healing take place are supernatural things the Holy Spirit can work in you. Give God room to work and give Him time to explain it.
- Love. The greatest evidence of the Holy Spirit is God's love flowing through you. This love will conquer hostility, personal jealousy, insecurity, unfair treatment, false accusations, and anything else you face. Love is a great insulator and instigator. It will insulate you from things that can hurt you and will instigate you to act in ways that will benefit others. Love is hard work and difficult to do. Through surrender to the Holy Spirit, you'll see an increased evidence of your ability to love others, even your enemies.

Your Next Steps

Whatever you do, continue to provide room for God to work personal transformation in you. He's in the middle of helping you reflect His image. We reflect His image best through aggressive surrender and active obedience. Our actions allow Him access to create new things in us.

Continue to serve others with compassion. Focusing on others keeps us from micromanaging God's work in us. Serve where you are able. Build relationships with those whom others have forgotten. Coach the young person on how to live. Be involved.

Be the evidence of Acts 1:8. Believe that God is making you into someone that will help others. Don't look back at your history—look forward to your destiny. God can take years that have been wasted and redeem them in seconds. He can take mistakes we've made and turn them into talking points. You can become the influence of God on this earth. Through your surrender, you will be the evidence of the Holy Spirit.

The world will never be restored through humanity's glorification of itself. The world will never be changed by laws. It will never be redeemed by good works. The world we live in, for as long as we're alive, is desperate for the revealing of the sons and daughters of God. Through the Holy Spirit, we can be revealed as the people we were created to be. We can be the restorers of the earth when the Holy Spirit is revealed within us.

That is our purpose. It is our call. Let's be the evidence of God and change this world.

ABOUT THE AUTHOR

Jason grew up on a farm in North Dakota and is living proof that God can use anyone for His purpose. He has helped equip thousands of people to reach their communities by directing community events, focused on helping the poor. Jason lives with his wife in Missouri.
Please visit: *jasonmbachman.com* for tools to use this book in small groups or book clubs that will help participants make a difference in their communities.